Symmetric Neural Networks Theory: Explained

Seymour L. Purvis

© Seymour L. Purvis

ALL RIGHTS RESERVED, 2024

Abstract

Symmetric functions, which take as input an unordered, fixed-size set, find practical application in myriad physical settings based on indistinguishable points or particles, and are also used as intermediate building blocks to construct networks with other invariances. Symmetric functions are known to be universally representable by neural networks that enforce permutation invariance. However the theoretical tools that characterize the approximation, optimization and generalization of typical networks fail to adequately characterize architectures that enforce invariance.

This book explores when these tools can be adapted to symmetric architectures, and when the invariance properties lead to new theoretical findings altogether. We study and prove approximation limitations on the extension of symmetric neural networks to infinite-sized inputs, the approximation capabilities of symmetric and antisymmetric networks relative to the interaction between set elements, and the learnability of simple symmetric functions with gradient methods.

Contents

Abstract

List of Figures

1 **Introduction**   1
    1.1 Challenges of Symmetric Networks 2
    1.2 Summary of Contributions 3

2 **Preliminaries**   8
    2.1 Permutation Invariance 8
    2.2 DeepSets Architecture 9
    2.3 Empirical Risk Minimization 9
    2.4 Inner Products 10
    2.5 Symmetric Polynomials 11

3 **The Limit of Sets to Measures**   13
    3.1 Preliminaries 14
    3.2 From Set to Measure Functions 17
    3.3 Neural Functional Spaces for Learning over Measures 21

		3.4 Separation of S_1 from S_2	24

| | 3.5 | Separation of S_2 from S_3 . . . . | 31 |
| | 3.6 | Experiments . . . . | 33 |

4 Approximating symmetric functions with high interaction — 36

	4.1	Preliminaries	38
	4.2	One-dimensional Separation Result	40
	4.3	Interaction Separation Statement	48
	4.4	Proof of Lower Bound	59
	4.5	Proof of Upper Bound	71

5 Approximating antisymmetric functions with high interaction — 79

	5.1	Preliminaries	81
	5.2	Separation Statement	85
	5.3	Proof of Lower Bound	87
	5.4	Proof of Upper Bound	93

6 Learning a Single Symmetric Neuron — 100

	6.1	Preliminaries	101
	6.2	Analytic Expression for Population Loss	106
	6.3	Derivation of Gradient Flow ODE	107
	6.4	Bounding ODE Convergence	112
	6.5	Experiments	132

List of Figures

1.1 Neural Networks that enforce symmetry 2

3.1 Planted neurons for $m = 100$ (left two) and $m = 200$ (right two). The smooth neuron has weights sampled consistently with $\mathcal{F}_2$ while the regular neuron has weights sampled distinctly from the network initialization. 35

5.1 Example of Young diagram and conjugate partition 84

5.2 λ and $\lambda + \delta$ for λ doubly even. 90

6.1 The learning trajectory, over ten independent runs, of the three summary statistics in the case of our chosen loss function L 133

1 Introduction

Deep learning theory begins with universal approximation, and an optimist might hope that would be the end of it. In the limit of infinite data there would be no need to move beyond two-layer vanilla neural networks. But regardless of how large datasets become, practitioners still seek to apply some kind of prior knowledge to improve optimization and generalization.

Typically, this prior knowledge is adapted to nature of the data. Self-attention, for instance, appears to be the appropriate prior to handle sequence data [Vaswani et al. 2017]. But often, this prior knowledge takes the form of underlying symmetry.

Classically, image data greatly benefits from architectures that enforce equivariance to translation [LeCun et al. 1998]. Likewise, for graphs we enforce invariance to node relabeling [Scarselli et al. 2008], for molecules we enforce rotational invariance [Cohen et al. 2018], for fermionic wavefunctions we enforce antisymmetry [Moreno et al. 2021], and so on.

For sets, the appropriate geometric prior is permutation invariance [Zaheer et al. 2017; Qi et al. 2017; Santoro et al. 2017]. Set data occurs organically in settings of particle physics or population statistics. But permutation invariance is also an essential primitive to be applied inside of other architectures, most notably for graphs [Kipf and Welling 2016] and antisymmetric wavefunctions [Pfau et al. 2020]. So we see permutation invariant architectures as first-class citizens in their own right, worthy of explicit study.

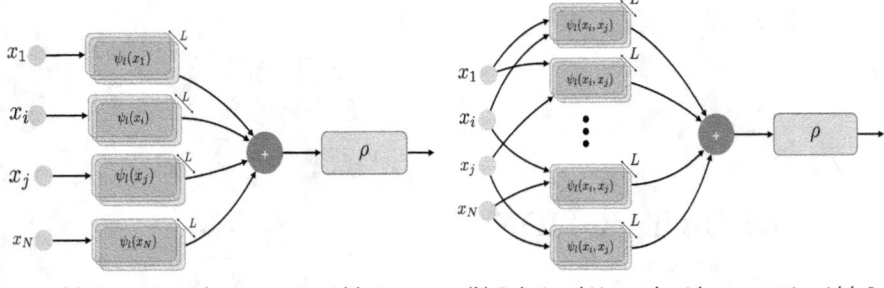

(a) DeepSets with symmetric width L **(b)** Relational Network with symmetric width L

Figure 1.1: Neural Networks that enforce symmetry

1.1 Challenges of Symmetric Networks

In some sense, permutation invariant networks provoke the same questions as vanilla networks. Namely, what functions can we approximate, when does gradient-based optimization succeed, and when do we successfully generalize?

These questions have been thoroughly explored for vanilla networks. To give only a cursory summary, great effort has been invested on the approximation capabilities of vanilla networks according to depth [Telgarsky 2016; Eldan and Shamir 2016; Daniely 2017; Safran and Shamir 2017; Venturi et al. 2021], the ability to learn a single neuron efficiently [Soltanolkotabi 2017; Frei et al. 2020; Yehudai and Shamir 2020; Wu 2022; Arous et al. 2021; Dudeja and Hsu 2018], and bounds on generalization [Neyshabur et al. 2017; Jiang et al. 2019].

The greatest quantitative progress on these questions for vanilla networks has been accomplished on two-layer networks, in part because this is the setting where high dimensional integrals may be calculated analytically. For finite networks, a common theme is relying on properties of Hermite polynomials [Arous et al. 2021] or spherical harmonics [Bach 2017] to calculate expectations over high-dimensional inputs, but this tactic breaks when handling the functions compositions inherent to deeper networks.

In general, moving towards higher depth networks, while not impossible, poses numerous difficulties. There is a smaller family of work considering deeper networks in the mean-field regime [Chen et al. 2022; Sirignano and Spiliopoulos 2022] in the limit of infinite widths. Pessimistically, the main theorem of [Vardi and Shamir 2020], dictates that depth separations above depth 4 would resolve long-standing open problems in circuit complexity, thought to be extremely difficult to address.

Two of the most common symmetric architectures are given in Figure 1.1, and notably they are both necessarily deeper than two layers. Although there are ways to enforce symmetry in two-layer networks [Bietti et al. 2021; Mei et al. 2021], this comes at a hefty cost to efficiency, so the typical architectures have at least three. This provokes substantial questions: when do the tricks for two-layer networks generalize? What new tactics are needed to understand this intermediate setting, with three layers but architectural restrictions that (in some cases) may make analysis easier?

Some works have broached lower bounds on the power of symmetric networks for one-dimensional inputs [Wagstaff et al. 2019, 2022]. Meanwhile, upper bounds on approximation either constructively require exponential size [Han et al. 2019a], or non-constructively show universality without quantitative bounds over the entire network [Wang et al. 2023; Dym and Gortler 2022]. But quantitative separations and learning guarantees remain unanswered questions.

1.2 SUMMARY OF CONTRIBUTIONS

This book is primarily concerned with the results of four papers [Zweig and Bruna 2021, 2022a,b, 2023] concerning different facets of symmetric neural networks.

MEASURE NETWORKS (CHAPTER 3): Motivated by symmetric functions defined over sets of any size, we consider when symmetric networks may be generalized to treat all sets as empirical measures, and therefore act on the space of probability measures itself. Under a simple continuity condition, we can characterize which functions are representable as neural networks acting on measures, where the dual product with test functions acts as a linear layer.

We observe three canonical function classes depending on which layers of the network are trained. Informally, these normed spaces include an RKHS S_3, the space of networks that only interact with measures through smooth test functions S_2, and the space of fully general networks S_1. Feature learning is essential for approximating some families of functions, and we therefore realize the following separation when the inputs are drawn from $\mathbb{R}^d$:

Theorem 1.1 (informal). *There exist f_1 with $\|f_1\|_{S_1} \leq 1$ and f_2 with $\|f_2\|_{S_2} \leq 1$ such that:*

$$\inf_{\|f\|_{S_3} \leq \delta} \|f - f_2\|_\infty \gtrsim d^{-2} \delta^{-5/d} \tag{1.1}$$

$$\inf_{\|f\|_{S_2} \leq \delta} \|f - f_1\|_\infty \gtrsim |d^{-11} - d^{-d/3}\delta| \tag{1.2}$$

APPROXIMATION SEPARATIONS (CHAPTER 4): We consider two variants of symmetric architectures: the class of networks which average over individual set elements Sym_L; or networks which average over pairs of set elements Sym_L^2. Here L is the symmetric width, which controls how many symmetric features the second half of the network takes as input (see Figure 1.1). Although universality cannot separate these networks when the width parameter $L \to \infty$, we can formalize the intuition that looking at pairwise interaction leads to more efficient representations.

Through the technical hammer of symmetric polynomial theory, we introduce an appropriate inner product to measure the expressiveness of these classes under the assumption of analytic activation functions.

The separation between these classes implies that singleton networks require exponentially many symmetric features in order to compete with pairwise networks, which justifies quadratic time spent in a forward pass of the latter.

Theorem 1.2 (informal). *Fix some non-trivial data distribution μ on $D \times N$ copies of the unit* complex circle $(S^1)^{D \times N}$. Then there exists an analytic symmetric function $g : \mathbb{C}^{D \times N} \to \mathbb{C}$ such that $\|g\|_{L_2(\mu)} = 1$ and the following is true:

For $L \leq N^{-2} \exp(O(\min(D, \sqrt{N})))$,

$$\min_{f \in Sym_L} \|f - g\|^2_{L_2(\mu)} \geq \frac{1}{12} \tag{1.3}$$

There exists a polynomially-sized $f \in Sym_L^\epsilon$ with $L = 1$ such that over $(S^1)^{D \times N}$:

$$\|f - g\|_\infty \leq \epsilon \tag{1.4}$$

ANTISYMMETRIC APPROXIMATION SEPARATIONS (CHAPTER 5): We focus now on the unusual invariance of antisymmetry, equivalent to symmetry up to a sign flip. This small change nevertheless has huge consequences for the architectures that enforce this property, and we consider two of the simplest architectures that are classical in quantum chemistry. Informally, these are the Slater ansatz, which is a sum of rank-one tensors projected into antisymmetric space; and the Jastrow ansatz, which is similar but augmented with a symmetric prefactor. In the interest of approximately solving Schrödinger's equation, we are motivated to understand when a more complicated model translates to more efficient representation.

When the symmetric prefactor is parameterized as a pairwise network, we are confronted with the a parallel question as Chapter 4, namely when allowing set elements (or in this case, electrons) to interact provably improves the approximation capacity of the function class. Again, enabling this interaction allows for an exponential improvement:

Theorem 1.3 (informal). *Assume an input domain with arbitrary $N > 1$ set elements that are each one-dimensional. Consider a Slater ansatz F with L terms and a Jastrow ansatz G with 1 term and a relational network as symmetric prefactor. Then there is a hard antisymmetric function G^* with*

$\|G^*\| = 1$, such that G is polynomially-sized and

$$\|G - G^*\|_\infty < \epsilon \tag{1.5}$$

but for $L \leq e^{N^2}$:

$$\min_F \|F - G^*\|^2 \geq \frac{3}{10} \tag{1.6}$$

SYMMETRIC SINGLE INDEX LEARNING (CHAPTER 6): We introduce a setting of symmetric single index models, a student-teacher model, where the student and teacher are both DeepSets architectures with fixed final layers. Equivalently, the teacher is a single neuron with inputs first mapped to fixed symmetric features. This is essentially the simplest setting for learning a family of non-trivial symmetric functions. By way of comparison, where the vanilla single index setting seeks to learn a function $x \mapsto f(\langle \theta^*, x \rangle)$, our setting considers a set of one-dimensional inputs and seeks to learn $x \mapsto f(\langle h^*, p(x) \rangle)$ where $p(x)$ is an infinite-dimensional vector of symmetric polynomials acting on x. In both cases, there is a notion of how non-linear f is, deemed the information exponent s.

Again, through symmetric polynomial theory it's possible to give analytic formulas for the population loss under very specific conditions, and even then one must choose a loss carefully to ensure the landscape, while non-convex, is nevertheless benign and easy to learn.

Consider a comparison to the vanilla single index model. There, using the population loss and under Gaussian inputs, the high-dimensional loss landscape can be simplified by only considering the correlation between the learned weight vector and the true hidden weight vector, reducing the problem to one-dimensional ODE where the correlation increases monotonically towards one [Arous et al. 2021]. Due to the three-layer nature of symmetric models, none of these facts hold true in our new setting, dramatically complicating the flow of the sufficient statistics that govern the loss. Nevertheless, we can still provably recover the hidden weight vector:

Theorem 1.4 (Informal). *Let $w \in \mathbb{C}^M$ be a learnable weight and $A \in \mathbb{C}^{\infty \times M}$ is a frozen weight matrix. Consider a correlational loss function L that only accesses h^* through $f(\langle h^*, p(z) \rangle)$, and is minimized when $Aw = h^*$. With constant probability under appropriate initialization, running gradient flow on $L(w)$ recovers h^* (up to phase) with ϵ accuracy in time*

$$T \leq \begin{cases} O\left(\log \frac{1}{\epsilon}\right) & s = 1 \\ O\left(2^{s^2} N^{7s} + \log \frac{1}{\epsilon}\right) & s > 1. \end{cases} \quad (1.7)$$

where s is the information exponent of f.

2 Preliminaries

2.1 Permutation Invariance

We will consider the following setup in the sequel: consider an input domain $\Omega \subseteq \mathbb{R}^D$ (or $\mathbb{C}^D$), and a set of N elements $X = \{x_1, \ldots x_N\}$ where $x_n \in \Omega$ for all $n \leq N$.

Then a function $f : \Omega^N \to \mathbb{R}$ (or $\mathbb{C}$) is symmetric if, for every permutation $\pi \in S_N$ acting on N elements,

$$f(x_1, \ldots x_N) = f(x_{\pi(1)}, \ldots, x_{\pi(N)}) \tag{2.1}$$

Equivalently, if one considers a matrix X of dimension $D \times N$, and assume f acts the set of its column vectors, the symmetry condition is equivalent to requiring that, for all permutation matrices $\Pi \in \mathbb{R}^{N \times N}$:

$$f(X\Pi) = f(X) \tag{2.2}$$

Traditionally, the algebra of continuous symmetric functions was considered in the context of symmetric polynomials. For real-valued functions, there are several canonical algebraic bases [Rydh 2007], and for complex-valued functions one must include symmetric Laurent polynomials in order to account for non-analytic functions.

2.2 DeepSets Architecture

Although there is more than one neural network architecture that is a universal approximator for the space of symmetric functions [Qi et al. 2017], in this work we will focus on DeepSets [Zaheer et al. 2017].

Definition 2.1. We consider the *DeepSets* architecture with symmetric width L, as functions f of the form:

$$f(X) = \rho(\phi_1(X), \ldots, \phi_L(X)) \qquad (2.3)$$

$$\phi_l(X) = \sum_{n=1}^{N} \psi_l(x_n) \qquad (2.4)$$

where $\{\psi_l : \Omega^D \to \Omega'\}_{l=1}^{L}$ and $\rho : (\Omega')^L \to \Omega''$ are arbitrary neural networks. Again, the domains Ω', Ω'' are either $\mathbb{R}$ or $\mathbb{C}$ depending on the setting.

Furthermore, in some cases we will use the notation $\Phi(X) = (\phi_1(X), \ldots, \phi_L(X))$ as the vector of all symmetric features in the network.

2.3 Empirical Risk Minimization

The motivating task for every problem we consider is learning a symmetric neural network from data. We mainly consider the regression setting for empirical risk minimization [Shalev-Shwartz and Ben-David 2014; Bach 2017], where given data $\{(X_i, f^*(X_i)\}_{i=1}^{n}$ with X_i drawn i.i.d. from some distribution over sets, we seek to learn

$$\hat{f} \in \arg\min_{f \in \mathcal{F}} \frac{1}{n} \sum_{i=1}^{n} \ell(f^*(X_i), f(X_i)), \qquad (2.5)$$

where $\mathcal{F}$ is a class of realizable DeepSets architectures, and ℓ is some convex loss (typically the squared loss).

2.4 Inner Products

Our choice of input distributions on sets will be motivated by the L_2 inner products they induce, and their associated properties. We introduce two L_2 inner products (defined with respect to probability measures) we'll use throughout the book.

For symmetric functions $f, g : \mathbb{C}^N \to \mathbb{C}$, define:

$$\langle f, g \rangle_V = \frac{1}{(2\pi)^N N!} \int_{[0, 2\pi]^N} f(e^{i\theta}) \overline{g(e^{i\theta})} |V(e^{i\theta})|^2 d\theta, \tag{2.6}$$

where for $z \in \mathbb{C}^N$, we have the Vandermonde determinant

$$V(z) = \prod_{1 \le i < j \le N} (z_j - z_i). \tag{2.7}$$

This inner product is well-known in the theory of symmetric polynomials, as a finite-variable analogue of the Hall inner product [Macdonald 1998]. Equivalently, if we let V denote the joint density of eigenvalues of a Haar-distributed unitary matrix in $\mathbb{C}^{N \times N}$, it is known [Diaconis and Shahshahani 1994] that this inner product may be written as

$$\langle f, g \rangle_V = \mathbb{E}_{y \sim V} \left[f(y) \overline{g(y)} \right]. \tag{2.8}$$

For arbitrary functions $f, g : \mathbb{C}^D \to \mathbb{C}$, we also consider the L_2 inner product given as an expectation over D random variables

$$\langle f, g \rangle_{S^1} = \frac{1}{(2\pi)^D} \int_{[0,2\pi]^D} f(e^{i\theta})\overline{g(e^{i\theta})} d\theta \qquad (2.9)$$

$$= \mathbb{E}_{q \sim (S^1)^D}\left[f(q)\overline{g(q)} \right], \qquad (2.10)$$

with the notation $q \sim (S^1)^D$ meaning each entry of q is i.i.d. uniform on S^1.

For this inner product, we will introduce the following notation. For a multi-index $\alpha \in \mathbb{N}^D$ and a dummy variable q of dimension D, we let q^α denote the polynomial function $z \mapsto z^\alpha$. Then orthogonality of the Fourier basis can be stated as the fact that

$$\langle q^\alpha, q^\beta \rangle_{S^1} = \mathbb{1}_{\alpha=\beta}. \qquad (2.11)$$

Note that we will consider this inner product over varying dimensions throughout the book, but it will be clear from context the dimension, i.e. how many i.i.d. random variables uniform on S^1 we are sampling over.

2.5 Symmetric Polynomials

The primary technical tool enabling fine-grained analysis of symmetric neural networks is the theory of symmetric polynomials [Macdonald 1998].

Definition 2.2. For $k \in \mathbb{N}$ and $x \in \mathbb{C}^N$, the *normalized powersum polynomial* is defined as

$$p_k(x) = \frac{1}{\sqrt{k}} \sum_{n=1}^{N} x_n^k$$

Definition 2.3. An *integer partition* λ is non-increasing, finite sequence of positive integers $\lambda_1 \geq \lambda_2 \geq \cdots \geq \lambda_k$. The weight of the partition is given by $|\lambda| = \sum_{i=1}^{k} \lambda_i$. The length of a partition $l(\lambda)$ is the number of terms in the sequence.

Then we characterize a product of powersums by:

$$p_\lambda(x) = \prod_i p_{\lambda_i}(x) \qquad (2.12)$$

Finally, define the combinatorial constant $t_\lambda = \prod_{i=1}^{|\lambda|}(m_i)!$ where m_i denotes the number of parts of λ equal to i.

The first significance of the powersum polynomials is that they form a natural to study the properties of the DeepSets architecture, as they obey the same simple structure of summing over all set indices to induce permutation invariance. The second significance of considering powersum products specifically, is that under a degree constraint, they form an orthogonal basis:

Theorem 2.4 ([Macdonald 1998, Chapter VI (9.10)]). *For partitions λ, μ with $|\lambda| \leq N$:*

$$\langle p_\lambda, p_\mu \rangle_V = t_\lambda \mathbb{1}_{\lambda=\mu} \qquad (2.13)$$

In symmetric polynomial theory, this theorem is typically stated under the assumption that x is a countable sequence of indeterminates, in which case partition size condition disappears and the powersums form a complete orthogonal basis over the space of symmetric polynomials.

This constraint on $|\lambda|$, or equivalently the degree of p_λ, arises from the restriction to sets of size N. Such a restriction is inescapable, as the fundamental theorem of symmetric polynomials [Macdonald 1998] dictates that $p_1, \ldots, p_N$ is a maximal algebraically independent set when x is of dimension N. So, for example, p_{N+1} can be written in the algebraic span of lower powersums, which contradicts orthogonality over all degree polynomials. Nevertheless, this limited orthogonality will suffice for decompositions of the DeepSets architecture.

3 THE LIMIT OF SETS TO MEASURES

For functions with invariance to permutation of the input elements, several universal architectures encode this invariance by treating the input as a set [Zaheer et al. 2017; Qi et al. 2017]. However, these formulations assume a constant input size, which precludes learning an entire family of symmetric functions.

Such symmetric functions appear naturally across several domains, including particle physics, computer graphics, population statistics and cosmology. Yet, in most of these applications, the input size corresponds to a sampling parameter that is independent of the underlying symmetric function of interest. As a motivating example, consider the function family induced by the max function, where for varying N, $f_N(\{x_1 \ldots x_N\}) = \max_{i \leq N} x_i$. It is natural to ask if a network can simultaneously learn all these functions.

In this chapter, we interpret an input set as an empirical measure defined over the base space Ω, and develop families of neural networks defined over the space of probability measures of Ω, as initially suggested in [Pevny and Kovarik 2019; De Bie et al. 2019]. We identify functional spaces characterized by neural architectures and provide bounds that showcase a natural hierarchy among spaces of symmetric functions. In particular, our framework allows us to understand the question of generalizing across input sizes as a corollary. Our constructions rely on the theory of infinitely wide neural networks [Bengio et al. 2006; Rosset et al. 2007; Bach 2017], and provide a novel instance of *depth separation* leveraging the symmetric structure of the input.

There is a wide literature considering neural networks that act on elements on functional data.

These results mainly consider universal approximation [Sandberg and Xu 1996; Stinchcombe 1999; Rossi and Conan-Guez 2005]. The work [Mhaskar and Hahm 1997] bears some similarity to the present topic, as they prove a quantitative separation between the class of neural networks and the class of functionals with bounded norm, while our main result shows separations among several neural network classes. Regarding variable input size, the work from [Wagstaff et al. 2019] proves lower bounds on representation of the max function in the DeepSets architecture with a dependency on input size.

A separate question concerns the approximation power of kernels constrained to respect permutation invariance. Previous work [Bietti et al. 2021; Mei et al. 2021] concerns the sample complexity of learning invariant functions, and demonstrates how kernels constrained to obey this invariance improve learning. However, for large groups such as the symmetric group, these models are made impractical by the need to project into the subspace of invariant functions, i.e. by averaging over all the group elements.

We consider the infinite-width limit of neural networks taking as domain the space of probability measures in order to formalize learning of symmetric function families. We prove a necessary and sufficient condition for which symmetric functions can be learned. By controlling the amount of non-linear learning, we partition the space of networks on measures into several function classes, proving a separation result among the classes.

3.1 Preliminaries

3.1.1 Convex Neural Networks

By considering the limit of infinitely many neurons [Bengio et al. 2006; Rosset et al. 2007], [Bach 2017] introduces two norms on shallow neural representation of functions ϕ defined over

$\mathbb{R}^d$. For a constant $R \in \mathbb{R}$, a fixed probability measure $\kappa \in \mathcal{P}(\mathbb{S}^d)$ with full support a signed Radon measure $\nu \in \mathcal{M}(\mathbb{S}^d)$, a density $p \in L_2(d\kappa)$, and the notation that $\tilde{x} = [x, R]^T$, define:

$$\gamma_1(\phi) = \inf\left\{\|\nu\|_{TV}; \phi(x) = \int_{\mathbb{S}^d} \sigma(\langle w, \tilde{x}\rangle)\nu(dw)\right\}, \text{ and} \quad (3.1)$$

$$\gamma_2(\phi) = \inf\left\{\|p\|_{L_2(d\kappa)}; \phi(x) = \int_{\mathbb{S}^d} \sigma(\langle w, \tilde{x}\rangle)p(w)\kappa(dw)\right\}, \quad (3.2)$$

where $\|\nu\|_{TV} := \sup_{|g|\leq 1} \int g d\nu$ is the *Total Variation* of ν and $\sigma_\alpha(t) = \max(0,t)^\alpha$ is the ReLU activation raised to the positive integer power α. These norms measure the minimal representation of ϕ, using either a Radon measure ν over neuron weights, or a density p over the fixed probability measure κ. The norms induce function classes:

$$\mathcal{F}_1 = \{\phi \in C_0(\Omega) : \gamma_1(\phi) < \infty\}, \text{ and } \mathcal{F}_2 = \{\phi \in C_0(\Omega) : \gamma_2(\phi) < \infty\}. \quad (3.3)$$

We also assume that the input domain Ω is bounded with $\sup_{x \in \Omega} \|x\|_2 \leq R$.

These two functional spaces are fundamental for the theoretical study of shallow neural networks and capture two distinct regimes of overparametrisation: whereas the so-called *lazy* or kernel regime corresponds to learning in the space $\mathcal{F}_2$ [Chizat and Bach 2018; Jacot et al. 2018], which is in fact an RKHS with kernel given by $k(x,y) = \mathbb{E}_{w\sim\kappa}\left[\sigma_\alpha(\langle w,\tilde{x}\rangle)\sigma_\alpha(\langle w,\tilde{y}\rangle)\right]$ [Bach 2017], the mean-field regime captures learning in $\mathcal{F}_1$, which satisfies $\mathcal{F}_2 \subset \mathcal{F}_1$ from Jensen's inequality, and can efficiently approximate functions with hidden low-dimensional structure, as opposed to $\mathcal{F}_2$ [Bach 2017]. Finally, we can consider the unit ball in these functional spaces, namely $\mathcal{A}_i = \{\phi \in \mathcal{F}_i : \gamma_i(\phi) \leq 1\}$ for $i = 1, 2$.

3.1.2 Spherical Harmonics and Kernel Norm Background

We'll use $\simeq$ to denote equality up to universal constants. To understand functions in $\mathcal{A}_2$, we require the following details of spherical harmonics [Efthimiou and Frye 2014].

A basis on $\mathbb{S}^d$ is given by the orthogonal polynomials $Y_{k,j}$, where $k \geq 0$ and $1 \leq j \leq N(d,k)$ where

$$N(d,k) \simeq \frac{k+d}{k}\frac{\Gamma(k+d-1)}{\Gamma(d)\Gamma(k)}$$
$$\simeq \frac{k+d}{k}\frac{(k+d)^{k+d-3/2}}{d^{d-1/2}k^{k-1/2}}$$

The Legendre polynomials $P_k(t)$ act on one dimensional real inputs and satisfy the addition formula

$$\sum_{j=1}^{N(d,k)} Y_{k,j}(x)Y_{k,j}(y) = N(d,k)P_k(\langle x,y \rangle)$$

Finally, given a function $g : \mathbb{S}^d \to \mathbb{R}$, the kth spherical harmonic of g is the degree k component of g in the orthogonal basis, equivalently written as

$$g_k(x) = N(d,k) \int_{\mathbb{S}^d} g(y)P_k(\langle x,y \rangle)\kappa(dy)$$

We also require several calculations on functions with bounded functional norm and projections [Bach 2017], where we remind that we're using the activation $\sigma(x)^2$. For $g \in \mathcal{A}_2$ or $g(x) = \sigma(\langle w,x \rangle)^2$ for any $w \in \mathbb{S}^d$, we have that $g_{2k} = 0$ for all $k \geq 2$.

For $g \in \mathcal{A}_2$, the norm of each harmonic satisfies $\|g_k\|_2^2 = \lambda_k^2 N(d,k)$, and the kernel norm can be calculated explicitly as

$$\gamma_2(g)^2 = \sum_{k=0, \lambda_k \neq 0}^{\infty} \lambda_k^{-2} \|g_k\|_{L_2}^2$$

We have that $\lambda_1 \simeq d^{-1}$, $\lambda_k = 0$ for $k \geq 3$ and k even, and for $k \geq 3$ and k odd:

$$\lambda_k \simeq \pm \frac{d^{d/2+1/2} k^{k/2-3/2}}{(d+k)^{k/2+d/2+1}} \tag{3.4}$$

3.2 From Set to Measure Functions

Suppose we consider a slight alteration to DeepSets where we average set elements instead of taking a sum, in order to keep magnitude independent of the number of set elements, i.e.

$$f_N(x) = \rho\left(\frac{1}{N} \sum_{n=1}^{N} \Phi(x_n)\right). \tag{3.5}$$

for $\Phi : \Omega \to \mathbb{R}^L$ and $\rho : \mathbb{R}^L \to \mathbb{R}$.

Universality is only proven for fixed N. Given a symmetric function $f \in \mathcal{F}$ we might hope to learn ρ and Φ such that this equation holds for all N. In other words, if we consider the powerset $\overline{\Omega} = \bigcup_{N=1}^{\infty} \Omega^N$, we might hope to define ρ and Φ such that we can define an extension $\overline{f}$ that acts on probability measures and agrees with f on any measure supported on $\overline{\Omega}$.

Treating the input to ρ as an average motivates moving from sets to measures as inputs, as proposed in [Pevny and Kovarik 2019; De Bie et al. 2019]. Given $x \in \Omega^N$, let $\mu^{(N)} = \frac{1}{N}\sum_{i=1}^{N} \delta_{x_i}$ denote the empirical measure in the space $\mathcal{P}(\Omega)$ of probability measures over Ω. Then (3.5) can be written as $f_N(x) = \rho\left(\int_\Omega \Phi(u) \mu^{(N)}(du)\right)$.

3.2.1 Continuous Extension

In general, the functions we want to represent don't take in measures $\mu \in \mathcal{P}(\Omega)$ as inputs. In this section, we want to understand when a function f defined on the power set $f : \overline{\Omega} \to \mathbb{R}$ can be extended to a continuous map $\bar{f} : \mathcal{P}(\Omega) \to \mathbb{R}$ in the weak topology, in the sense that for all $N \in \mathbb{N}$ and all $(x_1, \ldots x_N) \in \Omega^N$, $\bar{f}\left(\frac{1}{N}\sum_{i=1}^{N} \delta_{x_i}\right) = f(x_1, \ldots, x_N)$.

Observe that by construction $\bar{f}$ captures the permutation symmetry of the original f. Define the mapping $D : \overline{\Omega} \to \mathcal{P}(\Omega)$ by $D(x_1, \ldots, x_N) = \frac{1}{N}\sum_{i=1}^{N} \delta_{x_i}$. Let $\hat{\mathcal{P}}_N(\Omega) := D(\Omega^N)$ and $\hat{\mathcal{P}}(\Omega) = \bigcup_{N=1}^{\infty} \hat{\mathcal{P}}_N(\Omega)$, so that $\hat{\mathcal{P}}(\Omega)$ is the set of all finite discrete measures. For $\mu \in \hat{\mathcal{P}}(\Omega)$, let $N(\mu)$ be the smallest dimension of a point in $D^{-1}(\mu)$, and let x be this point (which is unique up to permutation). Then define $\hat{f} : \hat{\mathcal{P}}(\Omega) \to \mathbb{R}$ such that $\hat{f}(\mu) = f_N(x)$.

We also write $W_1(\mu, \mu')$ as the Wasserstein 1-metric under the $\|\cdot\|_2$ norm [Villani 2008]. The following proposition establishes a necessary and sufficient condition for continuous extension of f:

Proposition 3.1. *There exists a continuous extension $\bar{f}$ iff $\hat{f}$ is uniformly continuous with regard to the W_1 metric on its domain.*

Proof. We remind our notation. Given $f : \Omega \to \mathbb{R}$, the empirical extension $\hat{f} : \hat{\mathcal{P}}(\Omega) \to \mathbb{R}$ is defined as $\hat{f}(\mu) := f(x_\mu)$ where $x_\mu \in D^{-1}(\mu)$ and $\|x_\mu\|_0 = \min_{x \in D^{-1}(\mu)} \|x\|_0$. And for $\bar{f} : \mathcal{P}(\overline{\Omega}) \to \mathbb{R}$, we say this is a continuous extension of f if $\bar{f}$ is continuous in under the Wasserstein metric, and $f(x) = \bar{f}(D(x))$ for every real, finite-dimensional vector x.

For the forward implication, if $\bar{f}$ is a continuous extension, then clearly $\bar{f} = \hat{f}$ restricted to $\hat{\mathcal{P}}(\Omega)$.

Furthermore, continuity of $\bar{f}$ and compactness of $\mathcal{P}(\Omega)$ implies $\bar{f}$ is uniformly continuous, and therefore $\hat{f}$ is as well.

For the backward implication, we introduce $\hat{f}_\epsilon(\mu) = \sup_{\nu \in B_\epsilon(\mu) \cap \hat{\mathcal{P}}(\Omega)} \hat{f}(\nu)$ where the ball $B_\epsilon(\mu)$ is defined with the Wasserstein metric. Note that $\hat{f}_\epsilon$ is defined over arbitrary probability measures, not just discrete measures. Now, we introduce $\bar{f}(\mu) = \inf_{\epsilon > 0} \hat{f}_\epsilon(\mu)$, where density of the discrete measures and uniform continuity of $\hat{f}$ guarantees that $\bar{f}$ is well-defined and finite.

Uniform continuity implies if $\mu \in \hat{\mathcal{P}}(\Omega)$ then $\bar{f}(\mu) = \hat{f}(\mu)$. Consider any $y \in \Omega^M$ such that $\mu = D(y)$, and define a sequence of vectors $y^i = (z_i, y_2, \ldots, y_M)$ where $z_i \to y_1$ and all z_i are distinct from elements of y. Every point $y^i \in \Omega^M$ has a unique coordinate and therefore $\hat{f}(D(y^i)) = f_M(y^i)$. Because $D(y^i) \to D(y)$, continuity implies $\hat{f}(D(y)) = f_M(y)$. Thus, for any $y \in \Omega^M$, $\bar{f}(D(y)) = f_M(y)$, which implies $\bar{f}$ is an extension.

Now, suppose we have an arbitrary convergent sequence of probability measures $\mu_n \rightharpoonup \mu$. By the density of discrete measures, we can define sequences $\mu_n^m \rightharpoonup \mu_n$ where $\mu_n^m \in \hat{\mathcal{P}}(\Omega)$. In particular, we may choose these sequences such that for all n, $W_1(\mu_n^m, \mu_n) \leq \frac{1}{m}$. Then for any $\epsilon > 0$,

$$|\bar{f}(\mu) - \bar{f}(\mu_n)| \leq |\bar{f}(\mu) - \hat{f}_\epsilon(\mu)| + |\hat{f}_\epsilon(\mu) - \hat{f}(\mu_n^n)| + |\hat{f}(\mu_n^n) - \hat{f}_\epsilon(\mu_n)| + |\hat{f}_\epsilon(\mu_n) - \bar{f}(\mu_n)|.$$

Consider the simultaneous limit as $n \to \infty$ and $\epsilon \to 0$. On the RHS, the first term vanishes by definition, and the fourth by uniform continuity. For any $\nu \in B_\epsilon(\mu) \cap \hat{\mathcal{P}}(\Omega)$, $W_1(\nu, \mu_n^n) \leq W_1(\nu, \mu) + W_1(\mu, \mu_n) + W_1(\mu_n, \mu_n^n) \to 0$ in the limit. So the second term vanishes as well by uniform continuity of $\hat{f}$. Similarly, for any $\nu \in B_\epsilon(\mu_n) \cap \hat{\mathcal{P}}(\Omega)$, $W_1(\nu, \mu_n^n) \leq W_1(\nu, \mu_n) + W_1(\mu_n, \mu_n^n) \to 0$, and the third term vanishes by uniform continuity. This proves continuity of $\bar{f}$. □

This result formalises the intuition that extending a symmetric function from sets to measures requires a minimal amount of regularity across sizes. We next show examples of symmetric families that can be extended to $\mathcal{P}(\Omega)$.

3.2.2 Examples of Eligible Symmetric Families

MOMENT-BASED FUNCTIONS: Functions based on finite-range interactions across input elements admit continuous extensions. For example, a function of singleton and pairwise interactions

$$f(x) = \rho\left(\frac{1}{N}\sum_{i=1}^{N}\phi_1(x_i), \frac{1}{N^2}\sum_{i_1,i_2=1}^{N}\phi_2(x_{i_1},x_{i_2})\right)$$

is a special case of the continuous measure extension $\bar{f}(\mu) = \rho\left(\langle\phi_1,\mu\rangle, \langle\phi_2,\mu\otimes\mu\rangle\right)$ when $\mu = D(x)$.

RANKING: Suppose that $\Omega \subseteq \mathbb{R}$. The max function $f_N(x) = \max_{i\leq N} x_i$ cannot be lifted to a function on measures due to discontinuity in the weak topology. Specifically, consider $\mu = \delta_0$ and $\nu_N = \frac{N-1}{N}\delta_0 + \frac{1}{N}\delta_1$. Then $\nu_N \rightharpoonup \mu$, but for $\hat{f}$ as in Proposition 3.1, $\hat{f}(\nu_N) = 1 \neq 0 = \hat{f}(\mu)$.

Nevertheless, we can define an extension on a smooth approximation via the softmax, namely $g_N^\lambda(x) = \frac{1}{\lambda}\log\frac{1}{N}\sum_{i=1}^{N}\exp(\lambda x_i)$. This formulation, which is the softmax up to an additive term, can clearly be lifted to a function on measures, with the bound $\|g_N^\lambda - f_N\|_\infty \leq \frac{\log N}{\lambda}$. Although we cannot learn the max family across all N, we can approximate arbitrarily well for bounded N.

COUNTEREXAMPLES: Define the map $\Delta_k : \mathbb{R}^N \to \mathbb{R}^{kN}$ such that $\Delta_k(x)$ is a vector of k copies of x. Then a necessary condition for the function $\hat{f}$ introduced in Proposition 3.1 to be uniformly continuous is that $f_N(x) = f_{kN}(\Delta_k(x))$ for any k. Intuitively, if f_N can distinguish the input set beyond the amount of mass on each point, it cannot be lifted to measures. This fact implies any continuous approximation to the family $f_N(x) = x_{[2]}$, the second largest value of x will incur constant error.

3.3 Neural Functional Spaces for Learning over Measures

Equipped with knowledge of what kinds of symmetric functions can be understood as acting on general probability measures, we can define an appropriate neural network parameterization to learn them. We consider shallow neural networks that take probability measures as inputs, with test functions as weights.

Let $\mathcal{A}$ be a subset of $C_0(\Omega)$, equipped with its Borel sigma algebra. For $\mu \in \mathcal{P}(\Omega)$, and a signed Radon measure $\chi \in \mathcal{M}(\mathcal{A})$, define $f : \mathcal{P}(\Omega) \to \mathbb{R}$ as

$$f(\mu; \chi) = \int_{\mathcal{A}} \widetilde{\sigma}(\langle \phi, \mu \rangle) \chi(d\phi) \,. \tag{3.6}$$

where $\widetilde{\sigma}$ is again a scalar activation function, such as the ReLU, and $\langle \phi, \mu \rangle := \int_{\Omega} \phi(x) \mu(dx)$. Crucially, the space of functions given by $f(\cdot\, \chi)$ were proven to be dense in the space of real-valued continuous (in the weak topology) functions on $\mathcal{P}(\Omega)$ in [Pevny and Kovarik 2019; De Bie et al. 2019], and so this network exhibits universality.

Keeping in mind the functional norms defined on test functions in Section 3.1.1, we can introduce analogous norms for neural networks on measures. For a fixed probability measure $\tau \in \mathcal{P}(\mathcal{A})$, define

$$\|f\|_{1,\mathcal{A}} = \inf \left\{ \|\chi\|_{\text{TV}}; \tilde{f}(\mu) = \int_{\mathcal{A}} \widetilde{\sigma}(\langle \phi, \mu \rangle) \chi(d\phi) \right\}, \tag{3.7}$$

$$\|f\|_{2,\mathcal{A}} = \inf \left\{ \|q\|_{L_2}; f(\mu) = \int_{\mathcal{A}} \widetilde{\sigma}(\langle \phi, \mu \rangle) q(\phi) \tau(d\phi) \right\}, \tag{3.8}$$

where we take the infima over Radon measures $\chi \in \mathcal{M}(\mathcal{A})$ and densities $q \in L_2(d\tau)$. Analogously these norms also induce the respective function classes $\mathcal{G}_1(\mathcal{A}) = \{f : \|f\|_{1,\mathcal{A}} < \infty\}$, $\mathcal{G}_2(\mathcal{A}) = \{f : \|f\|_{2,\mathcal{A}} < \infty\}$. The argument in Appendix A of [Bach 2017] implies $\mathcal{G}_2(\mathcal{A})$ is an RKHS, with associated kernel $k_\mathcal{G}(\mu, \mu') = \int_{\mathcal{A}} \widetilde{\sigma}(\langle \phi, \mu \rangle) \widetilde{\sigma}(\langle \phi, \mu' \rangle) \tau(d\phi)$.

Moving from vector-valued weights to function-valued weights presents an immediate issue.

The space $C_0(\Omega)$ is infinite-dimensional, and it is not obvious how to learn a measure χ over this entire space. Moreover, our ultimate goal is to understand finite-width symmetric networks, so we would prefer the function-valued weights be efficiently calculable rather than pathological. To that end, we choose the set of test functions $\mathcal{A}$ to be representable as regular neural networks.

Explicitly, using the function norms of Section 3.1.1, we define

$$\mathcal{A}_{1,m} := \left\{\phi;\ \phi(x) = \sum_{j=1}^{m} \alpha_j \sigma(\langle w_j, \tilde{x}\rangle),\ \|w_j\|_2 \leq 1, \|\alpha\|_1 \leq 1\right\},$$

$$\mathcal{A}_{2,m} := \left\{\phi \in \mathcal{F}_{2,m} : \gamma_{2,m}(\phi) \leq 1\right\}.$$

$\mathcal{A}_{1,m}$ thus contains functions in the unit ball of $\mathcal{F}_1$ that can be expressed with m neurons, and $\mathcal{A}_{2,m}$ contains functions in the (random) RKHS $\mathcal{F}_{2,m}$ obtained by sampling m neurons from κ. By definition $\mathcal{A}_{2,m} \subset \mathcal{A}_{1,m}$ for all m. Representational power grows with m, and observe that the approximation rate in the unit ball of $\mathcal{F}_1$ or $\mathcal{F}_2$ is in $m^{-1/2}$, obtained for instance with Monte-Carlo estimators [Bach 2017; Ma et al. 2019]. Hence we can also consider the setting where $m = \infty$, with the notation $\mathcal{A}_{\{i,\infty\}} = \{\phi \in \mathcal{F}_i : \gamma_i(\phi) \leq 1\}$. Note also that there is no loss of generality in choosing the radius to be 1, as by homogeneity of σ any ϕ with $\gamma_i(\phi) < \infty$ can be scaled into its respective norm ball.

We now examine the combinations of $\mathcal{G}_i$ with $\mathcal{A}_i$:

- $\mathcal{S}_{1,m} := \mathcal{G}_1(\mathcal{A}_{1,m})$; the measure χ is supported on test functions in $\mathcal{A}_{1,m}$.

- $\mathcal{S}_{2,m} := \mathcal{G}_1(\mathcal{A}_{2,m})$; χ is supported on test functions in $\mathcal{A}_{2,m}$.

- $\mathcal{S}_{3,m} := \mathcal{G}_2(\mathcal{A}_{2,m})$; χ has a density with regards to τ, which is supported on $\mathcal{A}_{2,m}$.

- The remaining class $\mathcal{G}_2(\mathcal{A}_{1,m})$ requires defining a probability measure τ over $\mathcal{A}_{1,m}$ that sufficiently spreads mass outside of any RKHS ball. Due to the difficulty in defining this measure in finite setting, we omit this class.

Note that from Jensen's inequality and the inclusion $\mathcal{A}_{2,m} \subset \mathcal{A}_{1,m}$ for all m, we have the inclusions $\mathcal{S}_{3,m} \subset \mathcal{S}_{2,m} \subset \mathcal{S}_{1,m}$. And $\mathcal{S}_{3,m}$ is clearly an RKHS, since it is a particular instantiation of $\mathcal{G}_2(\mathcal{A})$. In the sequel we will drop the subscript m and simply write $\mathcal{A}_i$ and $\mathcal{S}_i$.

These functional spaces provide an increasing level of adaptivity: while $\mathcal{S}_2$ is able to adapt by selecting 'useful' test functions ϕ, it is limited to smooth test functions that lie on the RKHS, whereas $\mathcal{S}_1$ is able to also adapt to more irregular test functions that themselves depend on low-dimensional structures from the input domain. We let $\|f\|_{\mathcal{S}_i}$ denote the associated norm, i.e. $\|f\|_{\mathcal{S}_1} := \|f\|_{1,\mathcal{A}_1}$.

FINITE-WIDTH IMPLEMENTATION: For any m, these classes admit a particularly simple interpretation when implemented in practice. On the one hand, the spaces of test functions are implemented as a single hidden-layer neural network of width m. On the other hand, the integral representations in (3.7) and (3.8) are instantiated by a finite-sum using m' neurons, leading to the finite analogues of our function classes given in Table 3.1. Specifically,

$$f(\mu) = \frac{1}{m'} \sum_{j'=1}^{m'} b_{j'} \widetilde{\sigma}\left(\frac{1}{m} \sum_{j=1}^{m} c_{j',j} \int \sigma_\alpha(\langle w_{j',j}, \tilde{x}\rangle) \mu(dx)\right)$$

One can verify [Neyshabur et al. 2015] that the finite-width proxy for the variation norm is given by

$$\|f\|_1 = \frac{1}{m'} \sum_{j'} |b_{j'}| \|\phi_{j'}\|_1 \leq \frac{1}{mm'} \sum_{j',j} |b_{j'}| |c_{j',j}| \|w_{j',j}\|,$$

which in our case corresponds to the so-called path norm [Neyshabur et al. 2014]. In particular, under the practical assumption that the test functions $\phi_{j'}$ are parameterized by two-layer networks with shared first layer, the weight vectors $w_{j',j}$ only depend on j and this norm may be easily calculated as a matrix product of the network weights. We can control this term by constraining the weights of the first two layers to obey our theoretical assumptions (of bounded weights and test functions in respective RKHS balls), and regularize the final network weights.

	First Layer	Second Layer	Third Layer
S_1	Trained	Trained	Trained
S_2	Frozen	Trained	Trained
S_3	Frozen	Frozen	Trained

Table 3.1: Training for finite function approximation

3.4 Separation of S_1 from S_2

Our goal in this section is to demonstrate the superior approximation power of using general test functions rather than ones restricted to an RKHS.

For the remainder of this chapter, we consider $\tilde{\sigma} = \sigma$ as the ReLU activation, and choose $\alpha = 2$ such that $\sigma_2(t) = \sigma(t)^2$ is the squared ReLU.

Theorem 3.2. *There is some measure network f_1 such that we have $\|f_1\|_{S_1} \lesssim 1$, and*

$$\inf_{\|f\|_{S_2} \leq \delta} \|f - f_1\|_\infty \gtrsim |d^{-11} - d^{-d/3}\delta| \tag{3.9}$$

Let $g(x) = \sigma(\langle x, w \rangle)^2$ for an arbitrary $w \in \mathbb{S}^d$, we have that $\|g_k\|_2^2 = \lambda_k^2 N(d, k)$. Define $\tilde{g} = g - \sum_{i=0}^{d^2-1} g_i$.

The following lemmas capture that $\tilde{g}$ has high correlation with g and exponentially small correlation with functions in $\mathcal{A}_2$.

Lemma 3.3. *The correlation lower bound $\langle g, \tilde{g} \rangle \gtrsim d^{-21/2}$ holds.*

Proof. Note that

$$\langle g, \tilde{g} \rangle = \sum_{k=d^2} \|g_k\|_2^2 = \sum_{k=d^2} \lambda_k^2 N(d, k) \tag{3.10}$$

We can calculate, because $k + d \leq 2k$:

$$\lambda_k^2 N(d,k) \simeq \frac{d^{d+1}k^{k-5}}{(d+k)^{k+d+2}} \cdot \frac{k+d}{k} \frac{(k+d)^{k+d-3/2}}{d^{d-1/2}k^{k-1/2}}$$

$$\simeq d^{3/2}k^{-7/2}(k+d)^{-7/2}$$

$$\gtrsim d^{3/2}k^{-7}$$

And therefore

$$\langle g, \tilde{g} \rangle \gtrsim \sum_{k=d^2}^{\infty} d^{3/2}k^{-7} \geq d^{3/2}\int_{d^2}^{\infty} k^{-7}dk \simeq d^{3/2}(d^2)^{-6}$$

which yields the desired lower bound.

$\square$

Lemma 3.4. *The value of the optimization problem*

$$\max_{\phi} \quad \langle \hat{\phi}, \tilde{g} \rangle_{L_2}$$

$$\text{s.t.} \quad \gamma_2(\phi)^2 \leq \delta^2$$

is upper bounded by $\delta \cdot d^{1/2-d/3}$

Proof. By orthogonality we may assume $\phi_k = \alpha_k \tilde{g}_k = \alpha_k g_k$, where $\alpha_k = 0$ for $k < d^2$. Then the problem is equivalently

$$\min_{\alpha} \quad -\sum_{k=d^c}^{\infty} \alpha_k \|g_k\|_2^2$$

$$\text{s.t.} \quad \sum_{k=d^2}^{\infty} \alpha_k^2 \lambda_k^{-2} \|g_k\|_2^2 \leq \delta^2$$

Taking λ as a Lagrangian multiplier yields the optimality condition $\alpha_k = (2\lambda)^{-1}\lambda_k^2$. Plugging this into the constraint and introducing notation S yields

$$(2\lambda)^{-2}S := (2\lambda)^{-2}\sum_{k=d^2}^{\infty}\lambda_k^2\|g_k\|_2^2 \leq \delta^2$$

Then the objective (returned to a maximum) obeys the bound

$$\sum_{k=d^2}(2\lambda)^{-1}\lambda_k^2\|g_k\|_2^2 = (2\lambda)^{-1}S$$

$$\leq \delta\sqrt{S}$$

So it remains to calculate S. Plugging in the value of $\|g_k\|_2^2$ gives

$$S = \sum_{k=d^2}^{\infty}\lambda_k^4 N(d,k)$$

We can give the form of each term, using that $k \geq d^2$:

$$\lambda_k^4 N(d,k) \lesssim d^{3/2}k^{-7}\frac{d^{d+1}k^{k-3}}{(d+k)^{k+d+2}}$$

$$\lesssim d^{3/2}k^{-7}\frac{d^{d+1}k^{k-3}}{k^{k+d+2}}$$

$$\lesssim d^{5/2}k^{-12}\left(\frac{d}{k}\right)^d$$

$$\lesssim d^{5/2}k^{-12}\left(\frac{d}{k^{1/2}}\cdot\frac{1}{k^{1/2}}\right)^d$$

$$\lesssim d^{5/2}k^{-12}k^{-d/2}$$

For sufficiently large d, we may ignore the lower terms and reduce the exponential term to

$k^{-d/3}$, then:

$$S \lesssim \sum_{k=d^2}^{\infty} k^{-d/3} \simeq \int_{d^2}^{\infty} k^{-d/3} \simeq d^{-1}(d^2)^{1-d/3}$$

The bound follows.

□

Let $h = g - g_0 - g_2$, and define $f_1(\mu) = d^{-1}c\langle\langle h, \mu\rangle\rangle$, remembering that we're using the regular ReLU for the measure network activation.

Lemma 3.5. $\|f_1\|_{S_1} \lesssim 1$.

Proof. It suffices to bound $\gamma_1(h)$, remembering that our test functions are defined using networks with the squared ReLU activation. Clearly $\gamma_1(g) \leq 1$ as it itself a single neuron. For the other terms, we can write the harmonics explicitly, using the fact that $P_0(t) = 1$ and $P_2(t) = \frac{(d+1)t^2 - 1}{d}$. Starting with the constant term g_0:

$$\begin{aligned} g_0(x) &= \int_{\mathbb{S}^d} g(y)\kappa(dy) \\ &= \int_{\mathbb{S}^d} \sigma(\langle w, y\rangle)^2 \kappa(dy) \\ &= \int_{\mathbb{S}^d} \sigma(y_1)^2 \kappa(dy) \\ &= \frac{1}{2(d+1)} \end{aligned}$$

Note that $\sigma(z)^2 + \sigma(-z)^2 = z^2$, so we can represent a constant function as a neural network via:

$$\sum_{i=1}^{d+1} \sigma(\langle e_i, x\rangle)^2 + \sigma(\langle -e_i, x\rangle)^2 = \sum_{i=1}^{d+1} \langle e_i, x\rangle^2$$
$$= \|x\|_2 = 1$$

So we have $\gamma_1(g_0) \le 1$.

The second spherical harmonic is given as:

$$g_2(x) = N(d, 2) \int_{\mathbb{S}^d} g(y) \frac{(d+1)\langle x, y\rangle^2 - 1}{d} \kappa(dy)$$
$$= \frac{N(d,2)}{d} \left((d+1) \int_{\mathbb{S}^d} g(y)\langle x, y\rangle^2 \kappa(dy) - \int_{\mathbb{S}^d} g(y)\kappa(dy) \right)$$

We can represent the constant term as above, and the first integral as

$$\int_{\mathbb{S}^d} \sigma(\langle w, y\rangle)^2 \langle x, y\rangle^2 \kappa(dy) = \int_{\mathbb{S}^d} \sigma(\langle w, y\rangle)^2 (\sigma(\langle x, y\rangle)^2 + \sigma(\langle x, -y\rangle)^2)\kappa(dy)$$
$$= \int_{\mathbb{S}^d} \sigma(\langle x, y\rangle)^2 (\sigma(\langle w, y\rangle)^2 + \sigma(\langle w, -y\rangle)^2)\kappa(dy)$$
$$= \int_{\mathbb{S}^d} \sigma(\langle x, y\rangle)^2 \langle w, y\rangle^2 \kappa(dy)$$

This last line is a convex neural network representation using the squared ReLU activation, and thus we have $\gamma_1 \left(\int_{\mathbb{S}^d} g(y)\langle x, y\rangle^2 \kappa(dy) \right) \le \int_{\mathbb{S}^d} \langle w, y\rangle^2 \kappa(dy) = \frac{1}{d+1}$.

Thus, $\gamma_1(g_2) \le \frac{N(d,2)}{d}(1+1) \lesssim d$. And all together, $\gamma_1(h) \le \gamma_1(g) + \gamma_1(g_0) + \gamma(g_2) \lesssim d$.

So by homogeniety the bound on $\|f\|_{\mathcal{S}_1}$ follows.

□

Our choice of f_1 induces a separation between $\mathcal{S}_1$ and $\mathcal{S}_2$.

Proof of Theorem 3.2. Because we've subtracted out the 0th and 2nd harmonics, and all other even harmonics are zero, $\tilde{g}$ and h are odd functions.

Consider the signed measure $\nu(dx) := \frac{2\tilde{g}(x)}{\|\tilde{g}\|_{L_1}} \kappa(dx)$, with Jordan decomposition $\nu = \nu^+ - \nu^-$ with the positive measures $\nu^+(dx) := \frac{2\sigma(\tilde{g}(x))}{\|\tilde{g}\|_{L_1}} \kappa(dx)$ and $\nu^-(dx) := \frac{2\sigma(-\tilde{g}(x))}{\|\tilde{g}\|_{L_1}} \kappa(dx)$.

Note that from the oddness of $\tilde{g}$ and symmetry of κ:

$$TV(\nu^-) = \frac{2}{\|\tilde{g}\|_{L_1}} \int_{\mathbb{S}^d} \sigma(-\tilde{g}(x))\kappa(dx)$$
$$= \frac{2}{\|\tilde{g}\|_{L_1}} \int_{\mathbb{S}^d} \sigma(\tilde{g}(-x))\kappa(dx)$$
$$= \frac{2}{\|\tilde{g}\|_{L_1}} \int_{\mathbb{S}^d} \sigma(\tilde{g}(x))\kappa(dx)$$
$$= TV(\nu^+)$$

Because $TV(\nu^+) + TV(\nu^-) = TV(\nu) = 2$, we conclude ν^+ and ν^- are both probability measures. We'll use these measures to separate f and f_1. By Lipschitz continuity of σ:

$$|f(\nu^+) - f(\nu^-)| = \left| \int_{\mathbb{S}^d} \sigma(\langle \phi, \nu^+ \rangle) - \sigma(\langle \phi, \nu^- \rangle) \chi(d\phi) \right|$$
$$\leq \int_{\mathbb{S}^d} |\sigma(\langle \phi, \nu + \nu^- \rangle) - \sigma(\langle \phi, \nu^- \rangle)| \chi(d\phi)$$
$$\leq \sup_{\gamma_2(\phi) \leq 1} |\langle \phi, \nu \rangle| \|f\|_{S_2}$$
$$\leq \frac{2}{\|\tilde{g}\|_{L_1}} \sup_{\gamma_2(\phi) \leq 1} |\langle \phi, \tilde{g} \rangle| \|f\|_{S_2}$$
$$\lesssim \frac{2}{\|\tilde{g}\|_{L_1}} d^{1/2-d/3} \delta$$

where in the last line we use Lemma 3.4.

Concerning the function f_1, we first use oddness again to notice:

$$\langle h, v^- \rangle = \frac{2}{\|\tilde{g}\|_{L_1}} \int_{\mathbb{S}^d} h(x)\sigma(-\tilde{g}(x))\kappa(dx)$$
$$= \frac{2}{\|\tilde{g}\|_{L_1}} \int_{\mathbb{S}^d} h(x)\sigma(\tilde{g}(-x))\kappa(dx)$$
$$= \frac{2}{\|\tilde{g}\|_{L_1}} \int_{\mathbb{S}^d} h(-x)\sigma(\tilde{g}(x))\kappa(dx)$$
$$= -\langle h, v^+ \rangle$$

So $\langle h, v \rangle = \langle h, v^+ - v^- \rangle = 2\langle h, v^+ \rangle$, and therefore from Lemma 3.3 with $\alpha = 2$,

$$d^{-21/2} \lesssim \langle g, \tilde{g} \rangle = \langle h, \tilde{g} \rangle$$
$$= \frac{\|\tilde{g}\|_{L_1}}{2} \langle h, v \rangle$$
$$= \|\tilde{g}\|_{L_1} \langle h, v^+ \rangle$$

So $\langle h, v^+ \rangle \gtrsim \frac{d^{-21/2}}{\|\tilde{g}\|_{L_1}}$, and we conclude

$$|f_1(v^+) - f_1(v^-)| = d^{-1}|\sigma(\langle h, v^+ \rangle) - \sigma(\langle h, v^- \rangle)|$$
$$= d^{-1}\sigma(\langle h, v^+ \rangle)$$
$$\gtrsim \frac{d^{-23/2}}{\|\tilde{g}\|_{L_1}}$$

Now, suppose $\|f - f_1\|_\infty \leq \epsilon$. Then

$$\frac{d^{-23/2}}{\|\tilde{g}\|_{L_1}} \lesssim |f_1(v^+) - f_1(v^-)|$$

$$\leq |f_1(v^+) - f(v^+)| + |f(v^+) - f(v^-)| + |f(v^-) - f_1(v^-)|$$

$$\lesssim \epsilon + \frac{2}{\|\tilde{g}\|_{L_1}} d^{1/2 - d/3} \delta + \epsilon$$

So for sufficiently large d, we have $\frac{|d^{-23/2} - d^{1/2 - d/3}\delta|}{\|\tilde{g}\|_{L_1}} \lesssim \epsilon$. Finally, note by Jensen's inequality and spherical harmonic orthogonality that $\|\tilde{g}\|_{L_1} \leq \|\tilde{g}\|_{L_2} \leq \|g\|_{L_2} \lesssim d^{-1/2}$.

□

3.5 Separation of $\mathcal{S}_2$ from $\mathcal{S}_3$

The goal of this section is to show an analogous separation result, reiterating that feature learning is necessary even in the case of measure networks, rather than just learning in an RKHS space of measure-input functions.

In order to instantiate the class $\mathcal{S}_3$, we must fix τ, the base probability measure over test functions in $\mathcal{A}_2$. Consider some probability distribution ζ over the square-summable sequences $l_2(\mathbb{R}^+)$ such that for $c \in supp(\zeta)$, $\sum_{k=0}^\infty c_k^2 = 1$. Furthermore, we will make the simplyfing assumption that $c_0 = 0$. For each k let κ_k be uniform over $\mathbb{S}^{N(d,k)-1}$, and note that $N(d,1) = d+1$ so $\kappa = \kappa_1$. Then we sample $\phi \sim \tau$ as $\phi = \sum_{k=1}^\infty \sum_{j=0}^{N(d,k)} \lambda_k c_k \alpha_{kj} Y_{kj}$ where $c \sim \zeta$ and $\alpha_k \sim \kappa_k$. Observe that

$$\gamma_2(\phi)^2 = \sum_{k=1, \lambda_k \neq 0}^\infty \sum_{j=1}^{N(d,k)} \lambda_k^{-2} \lambda_k^2 c_k^2 \alpha_{kj}^2 = 1$$

so τ indeed samples functions from $\mathcal{A}_2$.

We define $f_2(\mu) = \sigma(\langle g, \mu \rangle)$ where $g = \lambda_1 Y_{11}$. Clearly $\gamma_2(g)^2 = \lambda_1^{-2} \lambda_1^2 \|Y_{1,1}\|_{L_2}^2 = 1$, so $|f_2|_{\mathcal{S}_2} \leq 1$.

Theorem 3.6. We have that $\|f_2\|_{S_2} \leq 1$, and

$$\inf_{\|f\|_{S_3} \leq \delta} \|f - f_2\|_\infty \gtrsim d^{-2}\delta^{-5/d} \tag{3.11}$$

Proof. Consider the function $h(x) = \sum_{j=1}^{N(d,1)} \beta_{1,j} Y_{1,j}$ and measure $\mu_\beta^*(dx) = \frac{h(x)+\|h\|_\infty}{\|h+\|h\|_\infty\|_{L_1}} \kappa(dx)$ where μ_β^* is chosen to be a probability measure. Observe that

$$f_2(\mu_\beta^*) = \frac{\lambda_1}{\|h + \|h\|_\infty\|_{L_1}} \sigma(\langle e_1, \beta \rangle)$$

For a function $f \in S_3$ with density q with respect to τ, we have:

$$\begin{aligned} f(\mu_\beta^*) &= \int_{\mathcal{A}_2} \sigma(\langle \phi, \mu_\beta^* \rangle) q(\phi) \tau(d\phi) \\ &= \frac{\lambda_1}{\|h + \|h\|_\infty\|_{L_1}} \int_{l_2(\mathbb{R}^+)} \int_{\mathbb{S}^d} \sigma(\langle c_1\alpha_1, \beta \rangle) \hat{q}(c, \alpha_1) \kappa(d\alpha_1) \zeta(dc) \\ &= \frac{\lambda_1}{\|h + \|h\|_\infty\|_{L_1}} \int_{\mathbb{S}^d} \sigma(\langle \alpha_1, \beta \rangle) \left[\int_{l_2(\mathbb{R}^+)} c_1 \hat{q}(c, \alpha_1) \zeta(dc) \right] \kappa(d\alpha_1) \end{aligned}$$

where $\hat{q}$ marginalizes out all other α_k terms. Let $\tilde{q}(\alpha_1) = \int_{l_2(\mathbb{R}^+)} c_1 \hat{q}(c, \alpha_1) \zeta(dc)$. From the fact that $c_1 \leq 1$, and by Jensen's inequality, $\|\tilde{q}\|_{L_2(\kappa)} \leq \|\hat{q}\|_{L_2(\kappa \times \zeta)} \leq \|q\|_{L_2(\tau)}$.

Now we may appeal to a separation of test function representations acting on spherical inputs. From D.5 in [Bach 2017], there exists some $\beta \in \mathbb{S}^d$ such that

$$|\sigma(\langle e_1, \beta \rangle) - \int_{\mathbb{S}^d} \sigma(\alpha_1, \beta) \tilde{q}(\alpha_1) \kappa(d\alpha_1)\| \gtrsim \|\tilde{q}\|_{L_2}^{-5/d} \geq \|q\|_{L_2}^{-5/d}$$

Therefore

$$|f_2(\mu_\beta^*) - f(\mu_\beta^*)| \gtrsim \frac{\lambda_1}{\|h + \|h\|_\infty\|_{L_1}} \|q\|_{L_2}^{-5/d}$$

Finally, note that $\lambda_1 \simeq d^{-1}$, and by the addition formula and the fact $P_k(1) = 1$ for all k:

$$\|h + \|h\|_\infty\|_{L_1} \leq 2\|h\|_\infty$$
$$= 2 \max_{x \in \mathbb{S}^d} \sum_{j=1}^{N(d,1)} \beta_{1,j} Y_{1,j}(x)$$
$$\leq 2 \max_{x \in \mathbb{S}^d} \|\beta\|_2 \sqrt{\sum_{j=1}^{N(d,1)} Y_{1,j}(x)^2}$$
$$\leq 2N(d,1)$$
$$\lesssim d$$

So we arrive at the desired bound.

□

3.6 Experiments

We instantiate our three function classes in the finite network setting, as outlined in Table 3.1. We use input dimension $d = 10$. For the finite realization of S_1, we use first hidden layer size $m = 100$ and second hidden layer size $h = 100$. Crucially, after fixing the finite architecture representing S_1, we scale up the width by 10 for the models with frozen weights. That is, the first hidden layer in S_2, and both hidden layers in S_3, have width equal to 1000. Increasing the width makes the S_2 and S_3 models strictly more powerful, and this setup allows us to inspect whether a larger number of random kernel features can compensate for a smaller, trained weight in approximation. For each model, we use its associated functional norm for regularization.

Each network is trained on a batch of 100 input sets. For our data distribution we consider the base domain $\Omega = [-3,3]^d$, and the distribution over input measures ξ places all its mass on the uniform measure $U([-3,3]^d)$. We choose to train with $N = 4$, i.e. all networks train on input sets of size 4, and test on sets of varying size. From the results we can measure out-of-distribution generalization of finite sets. We observe that these input measures will typically concentrate for symmetric functions like the softmax in the limit of high dimension, and that an interesting open question is the behavior under repulsive symmetric measures like the squared Vandermonde density.

Following the proofs of Theorem 3.2 and Theorem 3.6, we instantiate the functions that realize these separations as a planted neuron f_1 and a smooth planted neuron f_2.

For all experiments we use the same architecture. Namely, for an input set $x = (x_1, \ldots, x_N)$, the network is defined as $f_N(x) = w_3^T \sigma(W_2 \frac{1}{N} \sum_{i=1}^N \sigma(W_1 \tilde{x}_i))$, where we choose the architecture as $W_1 \in \mathbb{R}^{h_1 \times d}$, $W_2 \in \mathbb{R}^{h_2 \times h_1}$, and $w_3 \in \mathbb{R}^{h_2}$. Here, $h_1, h_2 = 100$ for $\mathcal{S}_1$, $h_1 = 100$ and $h_2 = 1000$ for $\mathcal{S}_2$, and $h_1 = h_2 = 1000$ for $\mathcal{S}_3$. The weights are initialized with the uniform Kaiming initialization [He et al. 2015] and frozen as described in Table 3.1.

We relax the functional norm constraints to penalties, by introducing regularizers of the form $\lambda \|f_N\|_{\mathcal{S}_i}$ for λ a hyperparameter. Let $K(\cdot)$ map a matrix to the vector of row-wise squared norms, and let $|\cdot|$ denote the element-wise absolute value of a matrix. Then we calculate the functional norms via the path norm as follows:

- For $\mathcal{S}_1$, $\|f_N\|_{\mathcal{S}_1} = |w_3|^T |W_2| K(W_1)$

- For $\mathcal{S}_2$, we explicitly normalize the frozen matrix W_1 to have all row-wise norms equal to 1, then $\|f_N\|_{\mathcal{S}_2} = |w_3|^T K(W_2)$

- For $\mathcal{S}_3$, we normalize the rows of W_1 and W_2, which simply implies $\|f_N\|_{\mathcal{S}_3} = \|w_3\|_2$

We optimized via Adam [Kingma and Ba 2014] with an initial learning rate of 0.0005, for 5000 iterations. Under this architecture, all S_1, S_2 and S_3 functions achieved less than 10^{-15} training error without regularization on all objective functions on training sets of 100 samples.

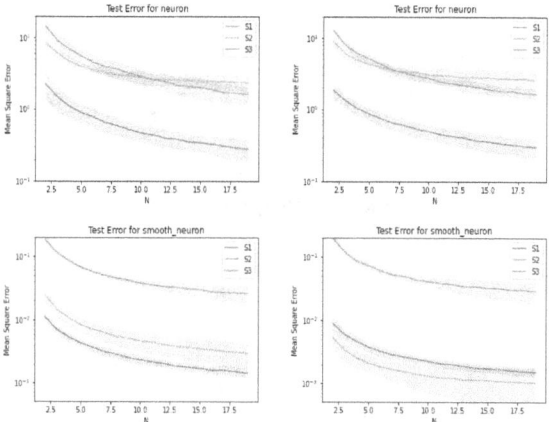

Figure 3.1: Planted neurons for $m = 100$ (left two) and $m = 200$ (right two). The smooth neuron has weights sampled consistently with $\mathcal{F}_2$ while the regular neuron has weights sampled distinctly from the network initialization.

The essential takeaway is the performance of the three models on the planted neurons in Figure 3.1. By using a distinct weight initialization for the neuron, its first layer will have very little mass under κ, and its first two layers will have little mass under τ, and therefore random features will not suffice to approximate this neuron. This is true even with the scaling of S_2 and S_3 to enable more random kernel features, reiterating that these single neuron functions realize a meaningful separation between the classes. We observe a more similar performance of S_1 and S_2 on the smooth_neuron, as this function is chosen to be exactly representable with the random kernel features sampled by S_2. According to the function class inclusion it is still representable by S_1, but from Theorem 3.6 not efficiently representable by S_3, which is consistent with the results.

4 Approximating symmetric functions with high interaction

The first symmetric architecture enabling explicit pairwise interaction was introduced in [Santoro et al. 2017], in the context of relationships between objects in an image. More complicated symmetric architectures, allowing for higher-order interaction and more substantial equivariant layers, were built on top of attention primitives [Ma et al. 2018; Lee et al. 2019]. And the notion of explicit high-order interactions between set elements before symmetrizing is formalized in the architecture of Janossy pooling [Murphy et al. 2018].

The question of expressiveness in symmetric networks may also be generalized to graph neural networks, with a focus on distinguishing non-isomorphic graphs as compared to the Weisfeiler-Lehman test[Xu et al. 2018] and calculating invariants such as substructure counting[Chen et al. 2020]. In particular, one may understand expressiveness in symmetric networks incorporating pairwise interaction as the ability to learn functions of the complete graph decorated with edge features.

Both the DeepSets and Relational Networks architectures are universal approximators for the class of symmetric functions. But empirical evidence suggests an inherent advantage of symmetric networks using pairwise interaction in synthetic settings [Murphy et al. 2018], on point cloud data [Lee et al. 2019] and in quantum chemistry [Pfau et al. 2020]. Intuitively, the increased complexity of calculating k-tuples should be rewarded with better approximation, but again the nature of these architectures is that three layers stymies easy analysis, and often one can only observe that they are all universal with sufficient depth and width.

Very careful geometric arguments can demonstrate that models with no interaction over 1-D elements cannot approximate some symmetric functions in the infinity norm unless network size scales linearly with set size [Wagstaff et al. 2022]. But this lower bound is not powerful enough to show superpolynomial advantages to using symmetric models with higher interaction. In a parallel but related line of work, [Sanford et al. 2023] proves bounds on shallow transformers based on the degree of interaction in the self-attention layers using a communication complexity argument.

Conversely, there are architectures that can demonstrate universal approximation while keeping the symmetric width parameter L polynomially small relative to the other problem parameters [Wang et al. 2023; Dym and Gortler 2022]. However, these results rely on non-constructive arguments that only guarantee approximation with a continuous network, without controlling the size of the networks overall.

In this chapter, we formalize this question in terms of approximation power, and explicitly construct symmetric functions which provably require exponentially-many neurons in the DeepSets model, yet are efficiently approximated with self-interaction. This exponential separation bears notable differences from typical separation results. In particular, while the expressive power of a vanilla neural network is characterized by depth and width [Eldan and Shamir 2016; Daniely 2017], expressiveness of symmetric networks with analytic activations is controlled particularly by a single parameter, the *symmetric width*. We observe the architectures with no interaction (even with arbitrary depth) require exponential symmetric width to match the expressive power of interacting architectures.

4.1 Preliminaries

We'll use $\mathbb{N}$ to denote the naturals including 0. The indicator function for the condition $x = y$ is written as $\mathbb{1}_{x=y}$. Given an integer *weak composition* $\alpha \in \mathbb{N}^D$, we will often consider the multidimensional polynomial $z^\alpha = \prod_{d=1}^{D} z_d^{\alpha_d}$. For two vectors $x, x' \in \mathbb{C}^D$, we denote their elementwise product by $x \circ x'$.

4.1.1 Symmetric Architectures

Given the *symmetric width* parameter L, we consider two primary symmetric architectures, as pictured in Figure 1.1:

Definition 4.1. Let Sym_L denote the class of *singleton symmetric networks* with symmetric width L, i.e. functions f of the form:

$$f(X) = \rho(\phi_1(X), \ldots, \phi_L(X)) \tag{4.1}$$

$$\phi_l(X) = \sum_{n=1}^{N} \psi_l(x_n) \tag{4.2}$$

where $\{\psi_l : \mathbb{C}^D \to \mathbb{C}\}_{l=1}^{L}$ and $\rho : \mathbb{C}^L \to \mathbb{C}$ are arbitrary neural networks with analytic activations.

The class Sym_L is exactly the architecture of DeepSets [Zaheer et al. 2017] restricted to analytic activations. However, we introduce this notation to differentiate this class from the more expressive architectures that allow for pairwise interaction among set elements.

From the theory of symmetric polynomials, if $L \geq L^* := \binom{N+D}{N} - 1$, then $f \in \mathrm{Sym}_L$ is a universal approximator for any analytic symmetric function [Rydh 2007]. Therefore we will primarily be interested in the expressive power of Sym_L for $L < L^*$.

Definition 4.2. Let Sym_L^2 denote the class of *pairwise symmetric networks* with symmetric width

L, i.e. functions f of the form:

$$f(X) = \rho(\phi_1(X), \ldots, \phi_L(X)) \tag{4.3}$$

$$\phi_l(X) = \sum_{n,n'=1}^{N} \psi_l(x_n, x_{n'}) \tag{4.4}$$

where $\{\psi_l : \mathbb{C}^{D \times D} \to \mathbb{C}\}_{l=1}^{L}$ and $\rho : \mathbb{C}^L \to \mathbb{C}$ are arbitrary neural networks with analytic activations.

Similarly, the class Sym_L^2 is exactly the architecture of Relational Pooling [Santoro et al. 2017] with analytic activations. We note this architecture is also equivalent to the 2-ary instantiation of Janossy Pooling [Murphy et al. 2018].

4.1.2 Multisymmetric Powersum Polynomials

When $D > 1$, in order to approximate our network with polynomials, we introduce the multivariate analog of symmetric polynomials. For example, suppose $D = 2$, and we write our set elements the following way:

$$X = \left\{ \begin{bmatrix} y_1 \\ z_1 \end{bmatrix}, \begin{bmatrix} y_2 \\ z_2 \end{bmatrix}, \ldots, \begin{bmatrix} y_N \\ z_N \end{bmatrix} \right\}$$

Then a basis of symmetric functions is given by the multisymmetric power sum polynomials, some examples:

$$p_{(2,3)}(X) = \frac{1}{\sqrt{2+3}} \sum_n y_n^2 z_n^3 \tag{4.5}$$

$$p_{(4,1)}(X) = \frac{1}{\sqrt{4+1}} \sum_n y_n^4 z_n^1 . \tag{4.6}$$

For general N and D, our input is $X \in \mathbb{C}^{D \times N}$ where we want functions that are invariant to permuting the columns x_n of this matrix. Note that we write scalar entries of this matrix as x_{dn}.

Definition 4.3. For a multi-index $\alpha \in \mathbb{N}^D$, the *normalized multisymmetric powersum polynomial* is defined as:

$$p_\alpha(X) = \frac{1}{\sqrt{|\alpha|}} \sum_n x_n^\alpha \qquad (4.7)$$

$$= \frac{1}{\sqrt{|\alpha|}} \sum_n \prod_d x_{dn}^{\alpha_d} \qquad (4.8)$$

with $p_0 = 1$.

An algebraic basis of symmetric functions in this setting is given by all p_α for all $|\alpha| \leq N$, where $|\alpha| = \sum_d \alpha_d$ (for a proof see [Rydh 2007]).

We remind the notation where $L^*(N, D) = |\{\alpha \in \mathbb{N}^D : 0 < |\alpha| \leq N\}| = \binom{N+D}{N} - 1$ is the size of this algebraic basis (discounting the constant polynomial). Intuitively then it's clear why $L \geq L^*$ will make Sym_L a universal approximator, as each of the L symmetric features $\{\phi_l\}_{l=1}^L$ will calculate one of these basis elements.

4.2 One-dimensional Separation Result

To begin, we consider the simpler case where $D = 1$, i.e. where we learn a symmetric function acting on a set of scalars. It was already observed in [Zaheer et al. 2017] that the universality of DeepSets could be demonstrated by approximating the network with symmetric polynomials. We first demonstrate that through this approximation, we can relate the symmetric width L to expressive power.

4.2.1 Projection Lemma

Before we can proceed to prove a representational lower bound, we need one tool to better understand $f \in \text{Sym}_L$. Utilizing the orthogonality properties of the inner product $\langle \cdot, \cdot \rangle_V$ allows us to project any $f \in \text{Sym}_L$ to a simplified form, while keeping a straightforward dependence on L.

For example, consider some uniformly convergent power series $\phi(x) = \sum_{i=1}^{\infty} c_{ik} p_k(x)$ with no constant term. We claim $\langle p_2 p_1, \phi^3 \rangle_V = 0$. Indeed, expanding ϕ^3, one exclusively gets terms of the form $p_{k_1} p_{k_2} p_{k_3}$, and because the partition $\{k_1, k_2, k_3\}$ is of a different length than $\{2, 1\}$, they are clearly distinct partitions so by orthogonality $\langle p_2 p_1, p_{k_1} p_{k_2} p_{k_3} \rangle_V = 0$.

Motivated by this observation, we can project f to only contain products of two terms. Let us introduce $\mathcal{P}_1$ to be the orthogonal projection onto $span(\{p_t : 1 \le t \le N/2\})$, and $\mathcal{P}_2$ to be the orthogonal projection onto $span(\{p_t p_{t'} : 1 \le t, t' \le N/2\})$.

Lemma 4.4. *Given any $f \in Sym_L$, we may choose coefficients v_{ij} over $i \le j \le L$, and symmetric polynomials ϕ_i over $i \le L$, such that:*

$$\mathcal{P}_2 f = \sum_{i \le j}^{L} v_{ij} (\mathcal{P}_1 \phi_i)(\mathcal{P}_1 \phi_j) . \tag{4.9}$$

Proof. Consider the general parameterization of f given in Equation 4.1. Because all network activations are analytic, we can write all maps parameterizing f by power series.

Note that the inner product $\langle \cdot, \cdot \rangle_V$ integrates over a compact domain, therefore the projection $\mathcal{P}_2 f$ will be determined by the value of f restricted to that domain. Thus, all power series in the sequel will converge uniformly and we may freely interchange infinite sums with each other as well as with inner products.

Explicitly, to parameterize f we write $\psi_l(x_n) = c_{l0} + \sum_{k=1}^{\infty} \frac{c_{lk}}{\sqrt{k}} x_n^k$ so that $\phi_l(x) = \sum_{n=1}^{N} \psi_l(x_n) = N c_{l0} + \sum_{k=1}^{\infty} c_{lk} p_k(x)$.

Because ρ is also given as a power series, it can be equivalently written as a power series with all variables having constant offsets. So we can subtract the constant terms from every ϕ_l and write:

$$\rho(y) = \sum_{\eta \in \mathbb{N}^L} v_\eta y^\eta, \qquad (4.10)$$

$$\phi_l = \sum_{k=1}^{\infty} c_{lk} p_k, \qquad (4.11)$$

where $y^\eta = \prod_{n=1}^{N} y_n^{\eta_n}$. Hence

$$f = \rho(\phi_1, \ldots, \phi_L) = \sum_{\eta} v_\eta \phi^\eta. \qquad (4.12)$$

We proceed to calculate $\mathcal{P}_2 f$. To begin, consider $\langle p_t p_{t'}, \phi^\eta \rangle$ for any choice of indices $1 \le t, t' \le N/2$. To illustrate, suppose $\eta_i = \eta_j = \eta_k = 1$ and η is 0 everywhere else. Then we may write

$$\langle p_t p_{t'}, \phi^\eta \rangle_V = \langle p_t p_{t'}, \phi_i \phi_j \phi_k \rangle_V = \sum_{i'=1}^{\infty} \sum_{j'=1}^{\infty} \sum_{k'=1}^{\infty} c_{ii'} c_{jj'} c_{kk'} \langle p_t p_{t'}, p_{i'} p_{j'} p_{k'} \rangle_V = 0. \qquad (4.13)$$

In other words, after distributing the product $\phi_i \phi_j \phi_k$, we are left with a sum of terms of the form $p_{i'} p_{j'} p_{k'}$. So treated as partitions, we clearly have $\{i', j', k'\} \ne \{t, t'\}$, where all these indices are positive. Thus, because $t + t' \le N$, we can apply the orthogonality property of the inner product to conclude $\langle p_t p_{t'}, p_{i'} p_{j'} p_{k'} \rangle_V = 0$.

By similar logic, $\langle p_t p_{t'}, \phi^\eta \rangle = 0$ whenever $|\eta| \ne 2$, so we may cancel all such terms in the expansion of f to get

$$\mathcal{P}_2 f = \mathcal{P}_2 \left(\sum_{\eta \in \mathbb{N}^L} v_\eta \phi^\eta \right) = \sum_{|\eta|=2} v_\eta \mathcal{P}_2 \phi^\eta.$$

Here we can simplify notation. Let $\{e_i\}_{i=1}^{L}$ denote the standard basis vectors in dimension L.

Every $\eta \in \mathbb{N}^L$ with $|\eta| = 2$ can be written as $\eta = e_i + e_j$, so let $v_{ij} := v_{e_i+e_j}$. Then we can rewrite:

$$\mathcal{P}_2 f = \sum_{i \leq j}^{L} v_{ij} \mathcal{P}_2 \phi_i \phi_j.$$

Finally, note again by orthogonality we have that $\mathcal{P}_2(p_{i'}p_{j'}) = 0$ if it is not the case that $1 \leq i', j' \leq N/2$. So observe that we may pass from $\mathcal{P}_2$ to $\mathcal{P}_1$:

$$\mathcal{P}_2 \phi_i \phi_j = \mathcal{P}_2 \left(\sum_{i'=1}^{\infty} c_{ii'} p_{i'} \right) \left(\sum_{j'=1}^{\infty} c_{jj'} p_{j'} \right) \tag{4.14}$$

$$= \mathcal{P}_2 \sum_{i'=1}^{\infty} \sum_{j'=1}^{\infty} c_{ii'} c_{jj'} p_{i'} p_{j'} \tag{4.15}$$

$$= \sum_{i'=1}^{N/2} \sum_{j'=1}^{N/2} c_{ii'} c_{jj'} p_{i'} p_{j'} \tag{4.16}$$

$$= \left(\sum_{i'=1}^{N/2} c_{ii'} p_{i'} \right) \left(\sum_{j'=1}^{N/2} c_{jj'} p_{j'} \right) \tag{4.17}$$

$$= (\mathcal{P}_1 \phi_i)(\mathcal{P}_1 \phi_j). \tag{4.18}$$

So ultimately we get

$$\mathcal{P}_2 f = \sum_{i \leq j}^{L} v_{ij} (\mathcal{P}_1 \phi_i)(\mathcal{P}_1 \phi_j). \tag{4.19}$$

□

4.2.2 Rank Lemma

Given the reduced form of f above, we may now go about lower bounding its approximation error to a given function g.

By the properties of orthogonal projection, we have $\|f - g\|_V^2 \geq \|\mathcal{P}_2(f - g)\|_V^2$. And by

Parseval's theorem, the function approximation error $\|\mathcal{P}_2 f - \mathcal{P}_2 g\|_V^2$ equals

$$\sum_{t \le t'} \left(\left\langle \mathcal{P}_2 f, \frac{p_t p_{t'}}{\|p_t p_{t'}\|_V} \right\rangle_V - \left\langle \mathcal{P}_2 g, \frac{p_t p_{t'}}{\|p_t p_{t'}\|_V} \right\rangle_V \right)^2.$$

Rearranging the orthogonal coefficients in the form of matrices, we have the following fact (stated very generally, since we will need to apply it later for a different commutative algebra than the one-dimensional powersums):

Lemma 4.5. *Consider a commutative algebra equipped with an inner product, and a set of elements $\{p_t\}_{t=1}^T$. Suppose the terms $p_{\{t,t'\}} = p_t p_{t'}$, indexed by sets $\{t, t'\}$, are pairwise orthogonal, and normalized such that*

$$\|p_t p_{t'}\|^2 \ge \begin{cases} 1 & t \ne t' \\ 2 & t = t' \end{cases}$$

Consider the terms:

$$\phi_l = \sum_{t=1}^T c_{lt} p_t,$$

$$f = \sum_{l \le l'}^L \frac{v_{ll'}}{1 + \mathbb{1}_{l=l'}} \phi_l \phi_{l'},$$

$$g = \sum_{t \le t'}^T \frac{g_{tt'}}{1 + \mathbb{1}_{t=t'}} p_t p_{t'}.$$

Then we have the bound

$$\|f - g\|^2 \ge \frac{1}{2} \|C^T V C - G\|_F^2, \tag{4.20}$$

where $C_{lt} = c_{lt}, V_{ll'} = v_{ll'}, G_{tt'} = g_{tt'}$, where we define V and G to be symmetric.

Proof. To begin, we calculate inner products for $t \neq t'$:

$$\left\langle f, \frac{p_{\{t,t'\}}}{\|p_{\{t,t'\}}\|} \right\rangle = \frac{1}{\|p_{\{t,t'\}}\|} \left\langle \sum_{l \leq l'}^{L} \sum_{t,t'=1}^{T} \frac{v_{ll'}}{1 + \mathbb{1}_{l=l'}} c_{lt} c_{l't'} p_t p_{t'}, p_t p_{t'} \right\rangle \tag{4.21}$$

$$= \|p_t p_{t'}\| \sum_{l \leq l'}^{L} \frac{v_{ll'}}{1 + \mathbb{1}_{l=l'}} (c_{lt} c_{l't'} + c_{lt'} c_{l't}) \tag{4.22}$$

$$= \|p_t p_{t'}\| \left(\sum_{l=l'}^{L} \frac{v_{ll}}{2} (c_{lt} c_{lt'} + c_{lt'} c_{lt}) + \sum_{l<l'}^{L} v_{ll'} (c_{lt} c_{l't'} + c_{lt'} c_{l't}) \right) \tag{4.23}$$

$$= \|p_t p_{t'}\| \left(\sum_{l=l'}^{L} v_{ll} c_{lt} c_{lt'} + \sum_{l<l'}^{L} v_{ll'} (c_{lt} c_{l't'} + c_{lt'} c_{l't}) \right). \tag{4.24}$$

Defining $v_{ll'} = v_{l'l}$, we may reindex and write the second sum as:

$$\sum_{l<l'}^{L} v_{ll'} (c_{lt} c_{l't'} + c_{lt'} c_{l't}) = \sum_{l<l'}^{L} v_{ll'} c_{lt} c_{l't'} + \sum_{l<l'}^{L} v_{ll'} c_{lt'} c_{l't} \tag{4.25}$$

$$= \sum_{l<l'}^{L} v_{ll'} c_{lt} c_{l't'} + \sum_{l>l'}^{L} v_{ll'} c_{lt} c_{l't'}. \tag{4.26}$$

So putting this together we get

$$\left\langle f, \frac{p_{\{t,t'\}}}{\|p_{\{t,t'\}}\|} \right\rangle = \|p_t p_{t'}\| \left(\sum_{l,l'}^{L} v_{ll'} c_{lt} c_{l't'} \right) = \|p_t p_{t'}\| [C^T V C]_{t,t'}.$$

By a similar calculation we conclude:

$$\left\langle f, \frac{p_{\{t,t\}}}{\|p_{\{t,t\}}\|} \right\rangle = \frac{\|p_t p_t\|}{2} [C^T V C]_{t,t}.$$

For g, we can directly calculate:

$$\left\langle g, \frac{p_{\{t,t'\}}}{\|p_{\{t,t'\}}\|}\right\rangle = \|p_t p_{t'}\| [G]_{t,t'} \tag{4.27}$$

$$\left\langle g, \frac{p_{\{t,t\}}}{\|p_{\{t,t\}}\|}\right\rangle = \frac{\|p_t p_t\|}{2} [G]_{t,t} . \tag{4.28}$$

Finally, by Parseval's Theorem we calculate:

$$\|f - g\|^2 = \sum_t \left(\left\langle f, \frac{p_{\{t,t\}}}{\|p_{\{t,t\}}\|}\right\rangle - \left\langle g, \frac{p_{\{t,t\}}}{\|p_{\{t,t\}}\|}\right\rangle\right)^2 + \sum_{t<t'}^T \left(\left\langle f, \frac{p_{\{t,t'\}}}{\|p_{\{t,t'\}}\|}\right\rangle - \left\langle g, \frac{p_{\{t,t'\}}}{\|p_{\{t,t'\}}\|}\right\rangle\right)^2 \tag{4.29}$$

$$= \sum_t \left(\left\langle f, \frac{p_{\{t,t\}}}{\|p_{\{t,t\}}\|}\right\rangle - \left\langle g, \frac{p_{\{t,t\}}}{\|p_{\{t,t\}}\|}\right\rangle\right)^2 + \frac{1}{2}\sum_{t\neq t'}^T \left(\left\langle f, \frac{p_{\{t,t'\}}}{\|p_{\{t,t'\}}\|}\right\rangle - \left\langle g, \frac{p_{\{t,t'\}}}{\|p_{\{t,t'\}}\|}\right\rangle\right)^2 \tag{4.30}$$

$$= \sum_t^T \frac{\|p_{\{t,t\}}\|^2}{4}[C^T V C - G]_{t,t}^2 + \frac{1}{2}\sum_{t\neq t'}^T \|p_{\{t,t'\}}\|^2 \cdot [C^T V C - G]_{t,t'}^2 \tag{4.31}$$

$$\geq \frac{1}{2}\sum_t^T [C^T V C - G]_{t,t}^2 + \frac{1}{2}\sum_{t\neq t'}^T [C^T V C - G]_{t,t'}^2 , \tag{4.32}$$

where in the last line we use our assumption on the lower bound of $\|p_{\{t,t'\}}\|^2$ and $\|p_{\{t,t\}}\|^2$. Hence:

$$\|f - g\|^2 \geq \frac{1}{2}\|C^T V C - G\|_F^2 . \tag{4.33}$$

$\square$

The significance of this lemma is the rank constraint: it implies that choosing symmetric width L corresponds to a maximum rank L on the matrix F. From here, we can use standard arguments about low-rank approximation in the Frobenius norm to yield a lower bound.

4.2.3 Separation in one-dimensional case

Our main goal in this section is to construct a hard symmetric function g that cannot be efficiently approximated by Sym_L for $L \leq N/4$. It is not particularly expensive for the symmetric width L

to scale linearly with the set size N; however, we will use the same proof structure to prove Theorem 4.8, which will require L to scale exponentially.

Theorem 4.6.

$$\max_{\|g\|_V=1} \min_{f \in Sym_L} \|f - g\|_V^2 \geq 1 - \frac{2L}{N}. \tag{4.34}$$

In particular, for $L = \frac{N}{4}$ we recover a constant lower bound.

Proof. We first build our counterexample g by choosing its coefficients in the powersum basis, say:

$$g = \frac{1}{\sqrt{N}} \sum_{t=1}^{N/2} p_t p_t . \tag{4.35}$$

From orthogonality and the fact that $\|p_t p_t\|_V^2 = 2$ it's clear that $\|g\|_V = 1$, and note that $\mathcal{P}_2 g = g$. Applying Lemma 4.4, for any $f \in Sym_L$ we can write $\mathcal{P}_2 f$ in the form

$$\mathcal{P}_2 f = \sum_{i \leq j}^{L} v_{ij} (\mathcal{P}_1 \phi_i)(\mathcal{P}_1 \phi_j) . \tag{4.36}$$

One may confirm that the Vandermonde inner product satisfies the requirements of Lemma 4.5 when restricted to the range of $\mathcal{P}_2$, owing to the orthogonality property and the fact that for $1 \leq t, t' \leq N/2$:

$$\langle p_t p_{t'}, p_t p_{t'} \rangle_V = \begin{cases} 1 & t \neq t' \\ 2 & t = t' \end{cases}$$

So we've met all the necessary requirements to apply Lemma 4.5 to $\mathcal{P}_2 f$ and $\mathcal{P}_2 g$, thus we have:

$$\min_{f \in \text{Sym}_L} \|f - g\|_V^2 \geq \min_{f \in \text{Sym}_L} \|\mathcal{P}_2 f - \mathcal{P}_2 g\|_V^2 \tag{4.37}$$

$$\geq \min_{C,V} \frac{1}{2} \|C^T V C - 2 * \frac{1}{\sqrt{N}} I\|_F^2 \tag{4.38}$$

$$= \min_{C,V} \frac{1}{N/2} \|C^T V C - I\|_F^2, \tag{4.39}$$

where the factor of 2 appears based on the definition of the matrix G in Lemma 4.5

Note that $CVC^T \in \mathbb{C}^{N/2 \times N/2}$, but $V \in \mathbb{C}^{L \times L}$. So if $N/2 > L$, then CVC^T is a rank-deficient approximation of the identity, and clearly we have

$$\min_{f \in \text{Sym}_L} \|f - g\|_V^2 \geq \frac{N/2 - L}{N/2} = 1 - \frac{2L}{N}. \tag{4.40}$$

□

4.3 Interaction Separation Statement

4.3.1 Theorem Statement

We state the main result, where for convenience we will change from N set elements to $2N$.

We introduce the notation $\hat{D} := \min\left(D, \lfloor \sqrt{N/2} \rfloor\right)$. We also introduce the L_2 inner product

$$\langle f, g \rangle_{\mathcal{A}} = \mathbb{E}_{y \sim V; q, r \sim (S^1)^D} \left[f(X(y, q, r)) \overline{g(X(y, q, r))} \right], \tag{4.41}$$

where the set input $X(y,q,r) \in \mathbb{C}^{D\times 2N}$ with matrix entries $x_{dn}(y,q,r)$ is defined by:

$$x_{dn}(y,q,r) = \begin{cases} q_d y_n & 1 \le n \le N, \\ r_d y_{n-N} & N+1 \le n \le 2N. \end{cases} \quad (4.42)$$

And we state an activation assumption in this new notation:

Assumption 4.7. The activation $\sigma : \mathbb{C} \to \mathbb{C}$ is analytic, and for a fixed D, N there exist two-layer neural networks f_1, f_2 using σ, both with $O\left(D^2 + D\log\frac{D}{\epsilon}\right)$ width and $O(D\log D)$ bounded weights, such that:

$$\sup_{|\xi|\le 3} |f_1(\xi) - \xi^2| \le \epsilon, \quad \sup_{|\xi|\le 3} \left| f_2(\xi) - \left(1 - (\xi/4)^{\min(D,\sqrt{N/2})}\right) \frac{\xi - 1/4}{\xi/4 - 1} \right| \le \epsilon \quad (4.43)$$

Essentially, this condition checks if a small network can approximate the square map and a rescaled Blaschke product. It is easy to confirm that, for example, the exp activation satisfies this assumption.

Then our main theorem is thus:

Theorem 4.8 (Exponential width-separation). *Fix $2N$ and D such that $\hat{D} > 1$, and consider set elements $X \in \mathbb{C}^{D\times 2N}$. Define*

$$g(X) = -\frac{4N^2}{4^{\hat{D}}} + \sum_{n,n'=1}^{2N} \prod_{d=1}^{\hat{D}} \left(1 - (x_{dn}x_{dn'}/4)^{\hat{D}}\right) \frac{x_{dn}x_{dn'} - 1/4}{x_{dn}x_{dn'}/4 - 1} \quad (4.44)$$

$$(4.45)$$

and $g' = \frac{g}{\|g\|_{\mathcal{A}}}$. Then the following is true:

- For $L \leq N^{-2} \exp(O(\hat{D}))$,

$$\min_{f \in Sym_L} \|f - g'\|_{\mathcal{A}}^2 \geq \frac{1}{12}. \tag{4.46}$$

- For $L = 1$, there exists $f \in Sym_L^2$, parameterized with an activation σ that satisfies Assumption 4.7, with width $poly(N, D, 1/\epsilon)$, depth $O(\log D)$, and maximum weight magnitude $O(D \log D)$ such that over the unit torus:

$$\|f - g'\|_{\infty} \leq \epsilon. \tag{4.47}$$

Remark 1. In the sequel, we will assume $D \leq \sqrt{N/2}$ so that $\hat{D} = D$. This is not a necessary assumption; in the case that $D > \sqrt{N/2}$, we can simply replace all instances of D with $\hat{D}$ in the definition of g and the subsequent proof. Because the data distribution has each row of $X \in \mathbb{C}^{D \times 2N}$ is i.i.d., the proof goes through exactly. Indeed, it would be equivalent to truncating each set vector to the first $\hat{D}$ elements. This will only impact the bounds by replacing D with $\hat{D}$.

To complete the theorem statement, we build the (unnormalized) hard function g, ultimately for the sake of Lemma 4.11. This lemma characterizes all the properties of g that we need to guarantee the lower and upper bounds.

4.3.2 MOBIUS TRANSFORM

We begin with the following, with $\xi \in \mathbb{C}$ and $|\xi| = 1$. And in the sequel, we always fix $r = 1/4$. Consider the 1-D Mobius transformation, with its truncated variant with $t \geq 1$:

$$\mu(\xi) = \frac{\xi - r}{r\xi - 1} \tag{4.48}$$

$$\hat{\mu}_t(\xi) = \left(1 - (r\xi)^t\right) \cdot \mu(\xi) \tag{4.49}$$

$$= (r - \xi) \cdot \left(1 + r\xi + (r\xi)^2 + \cdots + (r\xi)^{t-1}\right) \tag{4.50}$$

Lemma 4.9. *The following properties hold (where infinity norms are defined with respect to S^1):*

1. $\|\mu\|_\infty = 1$

2. $\|\mu\|_{S^1} = 1$

3. $\|\hat{\mu}_t\|_\infty \leq 1 + r^t$

4. $\|\hat{\mu}_t\|_{S^1}^2 = 1 + r^{2t}$

5. $\langle \hat{\mu}_t, 1 \rangle_{S^1} = r$, $\langle \hat{\mu}_t, \xi \rangle_{S^1} = r^2 - 1$ and $|\langle \hat{\mu}_t, \xi^a \rangle_{S^1}| < 1 - r^2$ for all $a \geq 2$

6. For $|\xi| = 1, |\omega| \leq 1 + \frac{1}{t}$,

$$|\hat{\mu}_t(\xi) - \hat{\mu}_t(\omega)| \leq 6|\xi - \omega| \tag{4.51}$$

Proof. It is a fact [Garnett 2007] that μ analytically maps the unit disk to itself, and additional the unit circle to itself, i.e. for any $|\xi| = 1$ we have $|\mu(\xi)| = 1$. Hence $\|\mu\|_\infty = \|\mu\|_{S^1} = 1$.

We can see that truncation gently perturbs this fact, so for $|\xi| = 1$:

$$|\hat{\mu}_t(\xi)| = |1 - (r\xi)^t| \cdot |\mu(\xi)| \tag{4.52}$$

$$\leq 1 + r^t \tag{4.53}$$

Additionally, we can calculate the coefficient on each monomial in $\hat{\mu}$:

$$\langle \hat{\mu}_t, \xi^a \rangle_{S^1} = \begin{cases} r & a = 0 \\ -(r^{a-1} - r^{a+1}) & 1 \leq a \leq t-1 \\ -r^{t-1} & a = t \\ 0 & a \geq t \end{cases} \tag{4.54}$$

It is easy to confirm that the value of $|\langle \hat{\mu}_t, \xi^a \rangle_{S^1}|$ is maximized at $a = 1$. Hence, we can write the L_2 norm:

$$\|\hat{\mu}_t\|_{S^1}^2 = \sum_{a=0}^{\infty} |\langle \hat{\mu}_t, \xi^a \rangle_{S^1}|^2 \tag{4.55}$$

$$= r^2 + \sum_{a=1}^{t-1} \left(r^{a-1} - r^{a+1}\right)^2 + r^{2t-2} \tag{4.56}$$

$$= r^2 + \sum_{a=1}^{t-1} \left(r^{2a-2} - 2r^{2a} + r^{2a+2}\right) + r^{2t-2} \tag{4.57}$$

$$= 1 + r^{2t} \tag{4.58}$$

Finally, for $|\xi| = 1, |\omega| \leq 1 + \frac{1}{t} \leq 2$:

$$|\mu(\xi) - \mu(\omega)| = \left| \frac{\xi - r}{r\xi - 1} - \frac{\omega - r}{r\omega - 1} \right| \tag{4.59}$$

$$= \left| \frac{(r^2 - 1)(\xi - \omega)}{(r\xi - 1)(r\omega - 1)} \right|. \tag{4.60}$$

So noting $r = \frac{1}{4}$ we get

$$|\mu(\xi) - \mu(\omega)| \leq \frac{8}{3}|\xi - \omega|. \qquad (4.61)$$

Thus:

$$|\hat{\mu}(\xi) - \hat{\mu}(\omega)| = \left|(1 - (r\xi)^t) \cdot \mu(\xi) - (1 - (r\omega)^t) \cdot \mu(\omega)\right| \qquad (4.62)$$

$$\leq \left|(1 - (r\xi)^t) \cdot \mu(\xi) - (1 - (r\omega)^t) \cdot \mu(\xi)\right| + \left|(1 - (r\omega)^t) \cdot \mu(\xi) - (1 - (r\omega)^t) \cdot \mu(\omega)\right|$$
$$\qquad (4.63)$$

$$\leq |\mu(\xi)| \cdot r^t |\xi^t - \omega^t| + |1 - (r\omega)^t| \cdot |\mu(\xi) - \mu(\omega)| \qquad (4.64)$$

$$\leq r^t |\xi^t - \omega^t| + |1 - (r\omega)^t| \cdot \frac{8}{3}|\xi - \omega|. \qquad (4.65)$$

Note that for $|\xi| = 1$, $|\omega| \leq 1 + \frac{1}{t}$, because $|\omega|^k \leq e$ for $k \leq t$, we have

$$\left|\xi^t - \omega^t\right| = \left|(\xi - \omega)(\xi^{t-1} + \xi^{t-2}\omega + \cdots + \xi\omega^{t-2} + \omega^{t-1})\right| \leq et|\xi - \omega|. \qquad (4.66)$$

Further plugging in that $r = \frac{1}{4}$ and $t \geq 1$:

$$|\hat{\mu}(\xi) - \hat{\mu}(\omega)| \leq 4^{-t} et |\xi - \omega| + (1 + 4^{-t}e) \cdot \frac{8}{3}|\xi - \omega| \qquad (4.67)$$

$$< 6|\xi - \omega|. \qquad (4.68)$$

$\square$

4.3.3 h FUNCTION

Now, consider $z \in \mathbb{C}^D$ with $|z_i| = 1$ for all i. We now define:

$$h(z) = \prod_{i=1}^{D} \hat{\mu}_D(z_i) . \tag{4.69}$$

Lemma 4.10. *The following are true:*

1. $\|h\|_\infty \leq 1 + 2^{-D}$

2. $1 \leq \|h\|_{S^1}^2 \leq 1 + 2^{-D}$

3. For $z, z' \in (S^1)^D$

$$|h(z) - h(z')| \leq 12\|z - z'\|_1 .$$

Proof. We can immediately bound:

$$\|h\|_\infty = \prod_{i=1}^{D} \|\hat{\mu}_D\|_\infty \tag{4.70}$$

$$\overset{(a)}{\leq} \left(1 + r^D\right)^D \tag{4.71}$$

$$\overset{(b)}{\leq} 1 + 2^D \cdot r^D \tag{4.72}$$

$$\leq 1 + 2^{-D} , \tag{4.73}$$

where (a) follows from Lemma 4.9.3 and (b) follows from the binomial identity that $(1 + x)^t \leq 1 + 2^t x$ for $x \in [0, 1], t \geq 1$. In the last line we simply plug in $r = 1/4$.

Similarly by Lemma 4.9.4,

$$\|h\|_{S^1}^2 = \prod_{i=1}^{D} \|\hat{\mu}_D\|_{S^1}^2 \tag{4.74}$$

$$= \left(1 + r^{2D}\right)^D \tag{4.75}$$

$$\leq \left(1 + r^D\right)^D. \tag{4.76}$$

And so by the same binomial inequality, we have

$$1 \leq \|h\|_{S^1}^2 \leq 1 + 2^{-D}. \tag{4.77}$$

Finally, observe that:

$$|h(z) - h(z')| \leq \sum_{i=1}^{D} \left|\left(\prod_{j=1}^{i-1} \hat{\mu}_D(z_j)\right) (\hat{\mu}_D(z_i) - \hat{\mu}_D(z_i')) \left(\prod_{j=i+1}^{D} \hat{\mu}_D(z_j')\right)\right| \tag{4.78}$$

$$\overset{(a)}{\leq} \sum_{i=1}^{D} \left|\hat{\mu}_D(z_i) - \hat{\mu}_D(z_i')\right| (1 + r^D)^{D-1} \tag{4.79}$$

$$\overset{(b)}{\leq} 6 \sum_{i=1}^{D} |z_i - z_i'| \left(1 + 2^{-D}\right) \tag{4.80}$$

$$\leq 12 \|z - z'\|_1, \tag{4.81}$$

where in (a) we apply 4.9.3, and in (b) we apply 4.9.6 and the same binomial identity as above. □

4.3.4 g FUNCTION

Now, reminding $z_{n,n'} = x_n \circ x_{n'}$, let:

$$g(X) = -4N^2 r^{\Gamma^a} + \sum_{n,n'=1}^{2N} h(z_{n,n'}). \tag{4.82}$$

Note that we subtract a constant here to ensure g has no constant term, which will be necessary for the fact $\mathcal{P}_2 g = g$.

Remark 2. The following lemma is the only place we explicitly require the assumption $D \leq \sqrt{N/2}$, as this guarantees that $\mathcal{P}_2 g = g$. In the case that $D > \sqrt{N/2}$, we simply replace all instances of D in this section with $\hat{D} = \min(D, \sqrt{N/2})$. This ensures g is only supported on $\mathbf{p}_{\{a,\alpha\}}$ with $|\alpha| \leq \hat{D}^2 \leq N/2$. And the subsequent proofs are identical.

Lemma 4.11. *The following are true:*

1. $\|g\|_\infty \leq 12N^2$.

2. $1 \leq \|g\|_{\mathcal{A}}^2 \leq 3N^2(1 + 2^{-D})$.

3. $\mathcal{P}_2 g = g$.

4. *We may write* $g = \sum_{1 \leq |\alpha| \leq N/2} g_\alpha \mathbf{p}_{\{a,\alpha\}}$, *where* $|g_\alpha|^2 \leq N^2(1 - r^2)^{2D}$.

5. $\mathrm{Lip}(g) \leq 48N\sqrt{ND}$.

Proof. First, it's easy to see from Lemma 4.10.1

$$\|g\|_\infty \leq |-4N^2 r^D| + 4N^2 \|h\|_\infty \tag{4.83}$$

$$\leq 4N^2 \left(2^{-2D} + 1 + 2^{-D}\right) \tag{4.84}$$

$$\leq 12N^2. \tag{4.85}$$

Let us expand h as

$$h(z) = \sum_{\|\alpha\|_\infty \leq D} h_\alpha z^\alpha, \tag{4.86}$$

noting that by definition of $\hat{\mu}_D$ and Lemma 4.9.5 we have the constant term $h_0 = r^D$.

Now we can expand

$$g(X) = -4N^2 r^D + \sum_{n,n'=1}^{2N} h(z_{n,n'}) \tag{4.87}$$

$$= -4N^2 r^D + \sum_{n,n'=1}^{2N} \left[r^D + \sum_{1 \leq \|\alpha\|_\infty \leq D} h_\alpha z_{n,n'}^\alpha \right] \tag{4.88}$$

$$= \sum_{n,n'=1}^{2N} \sum_{1 \leq \|\alpha\|_\infty \leq D} h_\alpha z_{n,n'}^\alpha \tag{4.89}$$

$$= \sum_{1 \leq \|\alpha\|_\infty \leq D} h_\alpha \sum_{n,n'=1}^{2N} \prod_{d=1}^{D} (x_{dn} x_{dn'})^{\alpha_d} \tag{4.90}$$

$$= \sum_{1 \leq \|\alpha\|_\infty \leq D} h_\alpha |\alpha| \left(\frac{1}{\sqrt{|\alpha|}} \sum_{n=1}^{2N} \prod_{d=1}^{D} x_{dn}^{\alpha_d} \right) \left(\frac{1}{\sqrt{|\alpha|}} \sum_{n'=1}^{2N} \prod_{d'=1}^{D} x_{d'n'}^{\alpha_{d'}} \right) \tag{4.91}$$

$$= \sum_{1 \leq \|\alpha\|_\infty \leq D} h_\alpha |\alpha| \mathbf{p}_{\{\alpha,\alpha\}}(X) . \tag{4.92}$$

Note that $\|\alpha\|_\infty \leq D$ implies $|\alpha| \leq D^2 \leq N/2$, so it clearly follows that $\mathcal{P}_2 g = g$. So by Lemma 4.12, $\langle \mathbf{p}_{\{\alpha,\alpha\}}, \mathbf{p}_{\{\beta,\beta\}} \rangle_\mathcal{A} = 12 \cdot \mathbb{1}_{\alpha=\beta}$ whenever $1 \leq |\alpha|, |\beta| \leq N/2$, so we can handily calculate:

$$\|g\|_\mathcal{A}^2 = \sum_{1 \leq \|\alpha\|_\infty \leq D} h_\alpha^2 |\alpha|^2 \|\mathbf{p}_{\{\alpha,\alpha\}}\|_\mathcal{A}^2 \tag{4.93}$$

$$\leq 12 \cdot (N/2)^2 \sum_{1 \leq \|\alpha\|_\infty \leq D} h_\alpha^2 \tag{4.94}$$

$$\leq 3N^2 \|h\|_{S^1}^2 \tag{4.95}$$

$$\leq 3N^2 \left(1 + 2^{-D}\right) , \tag{4.96}$$

where the last line uses Lemma 4.10.2.

And likewise

$$\|g\|_{\mathcal{A}}^2 = \sum_{1 \leq \|\alpha\|_\infty \leq D} h_\alpha^2 |\alpha|^2 \|\mathbf{P}_{\{a,\alpha\}}\|_{\mathcal{A}}^2 \tag{4.97}$$

$$\geq 12\left(-r^D + \sum_{\|\alpha\|_\infty \leq D} h_\alpha^2\right) \tag{4.98}$$

$$= 12(-r^D + \|h\|_{S^1}^2) \tag{4.99}$$

$$\geq 1, \tag{4.100}$$

and the last line again uses Lemma 4.10.2. Finally, note that for any α such that $|\alpha| \leq N/2$, applying Lemma 4.9.5.

$$|g_\alpha|^2 = |h_\alpha|\alpha||^2 = |\alpha|^2 \prod_{i=1}^{D} |\langle \hat{\mu}_D, \xi^{\alpha_i} \rangle_{S^1}|^2 \tag{4.101}$$

$$\leq N^2(1-r^2)^{2D}. \tag{4.102}$$

Finally we consider the Lipschitz norm. For $X, \hat{X} \in \mathbb{C}^{D \times 2N}$ with each entry of unit norm, it's easy to confirm by Lemma 4.10.3 that:

$$|g(X) - g(\hat{X})| \leq \sum_{n,n'=1}^{2N} |h(z_{n,n'}) - h(\hat{z}'_{n,n'})| \tag{4.103}$$

$$\leq 12 \sum_{n,n'=1}^{2N} \|z_{n,n'} - \hat{z}_{n,n'}\|_1 \tag{4.104}$$

$$= 12 \sum_{n,n'=1}^{2N} \sum_{d=1}^{D} |x_{dn}x_{dn'} - \hat{x}_{dn}\hat{x}_{dn'}| \tag{4.105}$$

$$\leq 12 \sum_{n,n'=1}^{2N} \sum_{d=1}^{D} |x_{dn}| \cdot |x_{dn'} - \hat{x}_{dn'}| + |\hat{x}_{dn'}| \cdot |x_{dn} - \hat{x}_{dn}| \tag{4.106}$$

$$= 48N \sum_{n=1}^{2N} \sum_{d=1}^{D} |x_{dn} - \hat{x}_{dn}| \tag{4.107}$$

$$= 48N \|X - \hat{X}\|_1 \tag{4.108}$$

$$\leq 48N \sqrt{2ND} \|X - \hat{X}\|_2 \tag{4.109}$$

□

4.4 PROOF OF LOWER BOUND

4.4.1 AN L_2 INNER PRODUCT

We must first motivate the chosen L_2 inner product, before we can prove a lower bound on function approximation. To that end, we will define an input distribution for the set inputs X.

Let us introduce several random variables: let $y \sim V$ as in the definition of the inner product $\langle \cdot, \cdot \rangle_V$ over N variables. Let q and r be two random vectors of dimension D, with each entry i.i.d. uniform on S^1.

Then we can define an input distribution for $X \in \mathbb{C}^{D \times 2N}$ with matrix entries x_{dn}:

$$x_{dn} = \begin{cases} q_d y_n & 1 \leq n \leq N \\ r_d y_{n-N} & N+1 \leq n \leq 2N . \end{cases} \qquad (4.110)$$

The point of this assignment is how it transforms multisymmetric power sums:

$$p_\alpha(X) = \frac{1}{\sqrt{|\alpha|}} \sum_{n=1}^{2N} \prod_d x_{dn}^{\alpha_d} \qquad (4.111)$$

$$= \frac{1}{\sqrt{|\alpha|}} \sum_{n=1}^{N} \prod_d y_n^{\alpha_d} q_d^{\alpha_d} + \frac{1}{\sqrt{|\alpha|}} \sum_{n=1}^{N} \prod_d y_n^{\alpha_d} r_d^{\alpha_d} \qquad (4.112)$$

$$= p_{|\alpha|}(y) \cdot (q^\alpha + r^\alpha) . \qquad (4.113)$$

Then consider the inner product:

$$\langle f, g \rangle_{\mathcal{A}} = \mathbb{E}_{y \sim V, q \sim (S^1)^D, r \sim (S^1)^D} \left[f(X) \overline{g(X)} \right] . \qquad (4.114)$$

From our choices above we may use separability to write $\langle \cdot, \cdot \rangle_{\mathcal{A}}$ in terms of previously introduced inner products. For example:

$$\langle p_\alpha, p_\beta \rangle_{\mathcal{A}} = \mathbb{E}_{y,q,r} \left[p_{|\alpha|}(y)(q^\alpha + r^\alpha) \overline{p_{|\beta|}(y)(q^\beta + r^\beta)} \right] \qquad (4.115)$$

$$= \mathbb{E}_y \left[p_{|\alpha|}(y) \overline{p_{|\beta|}(y)} \right] \mathbb{E}_{q,r} \left[(q^\alpha + r^\alpha) \overline{(q^\beta + r^\beta)} \right] \qquad (4.116)$$

$$= \langle p_{|\alpha|}, p_{|\beta|} \rangle_V \cdot \langle q^\alpha + r^\alpha, q^\beta + r^\beta \rangle_{S^1} . \qquad (4.117)$$

We can now observe this inner product grants a "partial" orthogonality:

Lemma 4.12. *Consider $\alpha, \beta \in \mathbb{N}^D$ with $1 \leq |\alpha|, |\beta| \leq N/2$. Then for $\gamma_k \in \mathbb{N}^D \setminus \{0\}$, if $K \neq 2$*

$$\left\langle p_\alpha p_\beta, \prod_{k=1}^{K} p_{\gamma_k} \right\rangle_{\mathcal{A}} = 0 . \tag{4.118}$$

Otherwise, for $K = 2$, we have:

$$\langle p_\alpha p_\beta, p_\gamma p_\delta \rangle_{\mathcal{A}} = 2 \cdot (1 + \mathbb{1}_{|\alpha|=|\beta|}) \cdot \mathbb{1}_{\{|\alpha|,|\beta|\}=\{|\gamma|,|\delta|\}} \cdot (\mathbb{1}_{\alpha+\beta=\gamma+\delta} + \mathbb{1}_{(\alpha,\beta)=(\gamma,\delta)} + \mathbb{1}_{(\alpha,\beta)=(\delta,\gamma)}) . \tag{4.119}$$

Proof. By separability, we can confirm that

$$\left\langle p_\alpha p_\beta, \prod_{k=1}^{K} p_{\gamma_k} \right\rangle_{\mathcal{A}} = \left\langle p_{|\alpha|} p_{|\beta|}, \prod_{k=1}^{K} p_{|\gamma_k|} \right\rangle_V \cdot C , \tag{4.120}$$

where C is the value of the expectation on the random variables q and r. Thus if $K \neq 2$, because $|\alpha| + |\beta| \leq N$, this term is 0 by orthogonality of the Vandermonde inner product.

For the $K = 2$ case, we begin again by using separability:

$$\langle p_\alpha p_\beta, p_\gamma p_\delta \rangle_{\mathcal{A}} = \left\langle p_{|\alpha|} p_{|\beta|}, p_{|\gamma|} p_{|\delta|} \right\rangle_V \cdot \left\langle (q^\alpha + r^\alpha)(q^\beta + r^\beta), (q^\gamma + r^\gamma)(q^\delta + r^\delta) \right\rangle_{S^1} . \tag{4.121}$$

Let's consider first the inner product of power sums. Plugging in the definition of the normalizing constant z_λ gives:

$$\left\langle p_{|\alpha|} p_{|\beta|}, p_{|\gamma|} p_{|\delta|} \right\rangle_V = (1 + \mathbb{1}_{|\alpha|=|\beta|}) \cdot \mathbb{1}_{\{|\alpha|,|\beta|\}=\{|\gamma|,|\delta|\}} .$$

Consider now the second inner product term. Noting that each element q_d, r_d is i.i.d. uniform on the unit circle, orthogonality of the Fourier basis implies we can calculate this inner product by only including terms with matching exponents. Bearing in mind that $\alpha, \beta, \gamma, \delta \neq 0$, we must always have terms of the form $\langle q^{\alpha+\beta}, q^\gamma r^\delta\rangle_{S^1} = 0$, and therefore we distribute and calculate:

$$\left\langle q^{\alpha+\beta} + q^\alpha r^\beta + q^\beta r^\alpha + r^{\alpha+\beta}, q^{\gamma+\delta} + q^\gamma r^\delta + q^\delta r^\gamma + r^{\gamma+\delta}\right\rangle_{S^1}$$
$$= \langle q^{\alpha+\beta}, q^{\gamma+\delta}\rangle_{S^1} + \langle q^\alpha r^\beta + q^\beta r^\alpha, q^\gamma r^\delta + q^\delta r^\gamma\rangle_{S^1} + \langle r^{\alpha+\beta}, r^{\gamma+\delta}\rangle_{S^1}$$
$$= 2 \cdot \mathbb{1}_{\alpha+\beta=\gamma+\delta} + 2 \cdot \mathbb{1}_{(\alpha,\beta)=(\gamma,\delta)} + 2 \cdot \mathbb{1}_{(\alpha,\beta)=(\delta,\gamma)}.$$

Collecting the terms of both products and evaluating the indicator functions under all cases gives the result. □

Looking at Equation 4.119, we can see inner product $\langle\cdot,\cdot\rangle_{\mathcal{A}}$ does not grant full orthogonality. The inner product gives orthogonality between powersum products of different lengths, but $\langle p_\alpha p_\beta, p_\gamma p_\delta\rangle_{\mathcal{A}}$ can be non-zero if $\alpha + \beta = \gamma + \delta$, even in the cases where $\{\alpha,\beta\} \neq \{\gamma,\delta\}$.

Nevertheless, this inner product still suffices to prove a similar result about projection for the $D > 1$ case.

Let $\mathcal{P}_1$ be the orthogonal projection onto $span(\{p_\alpha : 1 \leq |\alpha| \leq N/2\})$ and $\mathcal{P}_2$ be the orthogonal projection onto $span(\{p_\alpha p_\beta : 1 \leq |\alpha|,|\beta| \leq N/2\})$. Here by orthogonal, we mean with respect to $\langle\cdot,\cdot\rangle_{\mathcal{A}}$.

Lemma 4.13. *Given any $f \in Sym_L$ with $D > 1$, we may choose coefficients v_{ij} over $i \leq j \leq L$, and multisymmetric polynomials ϕ_i over $i \leq L$, such that:*

$$\mathcal{P}_2 f = \sum_{i \leq j}^{L} v_{ij}(\mathcal{P}_1 \phi_i)(\mathcal{P}_1 \phi_j). \tag{4.122}$$

Proof. As in Lemma 4.4, if we approximate $\psi_l(x_n) = c_{l0} + \sum_{\alpha \neq 0} \frac{c_{l\alpha}}{\sqrt{|\alpha|}} x_n^\alpha$, then symmetrizing gives $\phi_l(X) = N c_{l0} + \sum_{\alpha \neq 0} c_{l\alpha} p_\alpha$.

By a similar approximation as in Lemma 4.4 that allows us to subtract out constant terms, we write:

$$f = \sum_{\eta \in \mathbb{N}^L} v_\eta \phi^\eta, \qquad (4.123)$$

$$\phi_l = \sum_{\alpha \neq 0} c_{l\alpha} \mathbf{p}_\alpha . \qquad (4.124)$$

Note that by Lemma 4.12, $\langle \mathbf{p}_\alpha \mathbf{p}_\beta, \phi^\eta \rangle_{\mathcal{A}} = 0$ unless $|\eta| = 2$. So similarly to before, we may rewrite

$$\mathcal{P}_2 f = \sum_{|\eta|=2} v_\eta \mathcal{P}_2 \phi^\eta .$$

Here we can simplify notation. Let $\{e_i\}_{i=1}^{L}$ denote the standard basis vectors in dimension L. Every $\eta \in \mathbb{N}^L$ with $|\eta| = 2$ can be written as $\eta = e_i + e_j$, so let $v_{ij} := v_{e_i + e_j}$. Then we can rewrite:

$$\mathcal{P}_2 f = \sum_{i \leq j} v_{ij} \mathcal{P}_2 \phi_i \phi_j .$$

Again, by Lemma 4.12, we know $\mathcal{P}_2$ will annihilate any term of the form $\mathbf{p}_\gamma \mathbf{p}_\delta$ if it's not the case that $1 \leq |\gamma|, |\delta| \leq N/2$. One can see this by noting that, for $1 \leq |\alpha|, |\beta| \leq N/2$, then $\{|\alpha|, |\beta|\} \neq \{|\gamma|, |\delta|\}$, and by the Lemma, $\langle \mathbf{p}_\alpha \mathbf{p}_\epsilon, \mathbf{p}_\gamma \mathbf{p}_\delta \rangle_{\mathcal{A}} = 0$.

So we may pass from $\mathcal{P}_2$ to $\mathcal{P}_1$:

$$\mathcal{P}_2 \phi_i \phi_j = \mathcal{P}_2 \left(\sum_{\gamma \in \mathbb{N}^D} c_{i\gamma} \mathbf{p}_\gamma \right) \left(\sum_{\delta \in \mathbb{N}^D} c_{j\delta} \mathbf{p}_\delta \right) \tag{4.125}$$

$$= \mathcal{P}_2 \sum_{\gamma \in \mathbb{N}^D} \sum_{\delta \in \mathbb{N}^D} c_{i\gamma} c_{j\delta} \mathbf{p}_\gamma \mathbf{p}_\delta \tag{4.126}$$

$$= \sum_{1 \le |\gamma| \le N/2} \sum_{1 \le |\delta| \le N/2} c_{i\gamma} c_{j\delta} \mathbf{p}_\gamma \mathbf{p}_\delta \tag{4.127}$$

$$= \left(\sum_{1 \le |\gamma| \le N/2} c_{i\gamma} \mathbf{p}_\gamma \right) \left(\sum_{1 \le |\delta| \le N/2} c_{j\delta} \mathbf{p}_\delta \right) \tag{4.128}$$

$$= (\mathcal{P}_1 \phi_i)(\mathcal{P}_1 \phi_j) \,. \tag{4.129}$$

So ultimately we get

$$\mathcal{P}_2 f = \sum_{i \le j}^{L} v_{ij} (\mathcal{P}_1 \phi_i)(\mathcal{P}_1 \phi_j) \,. \tag{4.130}$$

□

4.4.2 A Diagonal Inner Product

Before we can apply Lemma 4.5, which lets us transform function approximation error into matrix approximation error, we need a better inner product, one that is diagonal in the low-degree multisymmetric powersum basis.

Consider two more inner products, defined for f, g in the range of $\mathcal{P}_2$:

$$\langle f, g \rangle_{\mathcal{A}_0} = \mathbb{E}_{y \sim V, q \sim (S^1)^D, r=0} \left[f(X) \overline{g(X)} \right] \,. \tag{4.131}$$

This is nearly the same distribution as before, except we fix $r = 0$.

Then define

$$\langle f, g \rangle_* = \langle f, g \rangle_{\mathcal{A}} - 2\langle f, g \rangle_{\mathcal{A}_0} . \qquad (4.132)$$

Because f and g are restricted to the range of $\mathcal{P}_2$, we demonstrate positive-definiteness of this object, and therefore it is a valid inner product.

Theorem 4.14. *The bilinear form $\langle \cdot, \cdot \rangle_*$ is an inner product when restricted to the range of $\mathcal{P}_2$. Furthermore, it is diagonal in the powersum basis $p_{\{\alpha,\beta\}}$ for $1 \leq |\alpha|, |\beta| \leq N/2$.*

Proof. Given $p_\alpha p_\beta, p_\gamma p_\delta \in im(\mathcal{P}_2)$, we can consider $\langle p_\alpha p_\beta, p_\gamma p_\delta \rangle_{\mathcal{A}_0}$ which can similarly be calculated via separability:

$$\langle p_\alpha p_\beta, p_\gamma p_\delta \rangle_{\mathcal{A}_0} = \langle p_{|\alpha|} p_{|\beta|}, p_{|\gamma|} p_{|\delta|} \rangle_V \cdot \langle q^{\alpha+\beta}, q^{\gamma+\delta} \rangle_{S^1}$$

$$= (1 + \mathbb{1}_{|\alpha|=|\beta|}) \cdot \mathbb{1}_{\{|\alpha|,|\beta|\}=\{|\gamma|,|\delta|\}} \cdot \mathbb{1}_{\alpha+\beta=\gamma+\delta} .$$

It follows from Lemma 4.12 that:

$$\langle p_\alpha p_\beta, p_\gamma p_\delta \rangle_* = \langle p_\alpha p_\beta, p_\gamma p_\delta \rangle_{\mathcal{A}} - 2\langle p_\alpha p_\beta, p_\gamma p_\delta \rangle_{\mathcal{A}_0}$$

$$= 2 \cdot (1 + \mathbb{1}_{|\alpha|=|\beta|}) \cdot (\mathbb{1}_{(\alpha,\beta)=(\gamma,\delta)} + \mathbb{1}_{(\alpha,\beta)=(\delta,\gamma)}) .$$

To eliminate the ambiguity of $p_\alpha p_\beta$ vs. $p_\beta p_\alpha$, let us define $p_{\{\alpha,\beta\}}$ equal to both these terms. Then we can equivalently write:

$$\langle p_{\{\alpha,\beta\}}, p_{\{\gamma,\delta\}} \rangle_* = 2 \cdot (1 + \mathbb{1}_{|\alpha|=|\beta|}) \cdot (1 + \mathbb{1}_{\alpha=\beta}) \cdot \mathbb{1}_{\{\alpha,\beta\}=\{\gamma,\delta\}} .$$

Evaluating the indicator functions under all cases we can see:

$$\langle p_\alpha p_\beta, p_\gamma p_\delta \rangle_* = \begin{cases} 0 & \{\alpha,\beta\} \neq \{\gamma,\delta\} \\ 2 & \{\alpha,\beta\} = \{\gamma,\delta\}, \quad |\alpha| \neq |\beta| \\ 4 & \{\alpha,\beta\} = \{\gamma,\delta\}, \quad |\alpha| = |\beta|, \quad \alpha \neq \beta \\ 8 & \{\alpha,\beta\} = \{\gamma,\delta\}, \quad \alpha = \beta \end{cases}$$

Then we've shown that the bilinear form $\langle \cdot, \cdot \rangle_*$, treated as a matrix in the basis of all $p_{\{\alpha,\beta\}}$, is positive-definite and diagonal. Since this basis spans the range of $\mathcal{P}_2$, it follows that the bilinear form is an inner product. □

4.4.3 Proof of Lower Bound

We first prove a lower bound using a slightly simpler hard function g, before updating the argument to the true choice of g further below.

Theorem 4.15. *Let $D > 1$. In particular, assume $\min(N/2, D-1) \geq 2$. Then we have*

$$\max_{\|g\|_{\mathcal{A}}=1} \min_{f \in \mathrm{Sym}_L} \|f - g\|_{\mathcal{A}}^2 \geq \frac{1}{6} - \frac{L}{6 \cdot 2^{\min(N/2, D-1)}} . \tag{4.133}$$

So for $L \leq 2^{\min(N/2, D-1)-3}$ we have a constant lower bound on the approximation error.

Proof. Define $T = |\{\alpha \in \mathbb{N}^D : |\alpha| = N/2\}|$ and choose the bad function $g = \frac{1}{\sqrt{12T}} \sum_{|\alpha|=N/2} p_{\{\alpha,\alpha\}}$.

Observe that although $\langle \cdot, \cdot \rangle_{\mathcal{A}}$ is not fully orthogonal in the powersum basis, we can nevertheless calculate by Lemma 4.12 that for $|\alpha| = |\beta| = N/2$:

$$\langle p_{\{\alpha,\alpha\}}, p_{\{\beta,\beta\}} \rangle_{\mathcal{A}} = 4 \cdot (\mathbb{1}_{\alpha+\alpha=\beta+\beta} + \mathbb{1}_{(\alpha,\alpha)=(\beta,\beta)} + \mathbb{1}_{(\alpha,\alpha)=(\beta,\beta)}) \tag{4.134}$$

$$= 12 \cdot \mathbb{1}_{\alpha=\beta} . \tag{4.135}$$

Therefore we can confirm that g is normalized:

$$\|g\|_{\mathcal{A}}^2 = \frac{1}{12T} \sum_{|\alpha|=N/2} \sum_{|\beta|=N/2} \langle \mathbf{p}_{\{\alpha,\alpha\}}, \mathbf{p}_{\{\beta,\beta\}} \rangle_{\mathcal{A}} \qquad (4.136)$$

$$= \frac{1}{12T} \sum_{|\alpha|=N/2} \sum_{|\alpha|=N/2} 12 \cdot \mathbb{1}_{\alpha=\beta} \qquad (4.137)$$

$$= \frac{1}{T} \sum_{|\alpha|=N/2} 1 \qquad (4.138)$$

$$= 1. \qquad (4.139)$$

Again, we have $\mathcal{P}_2 g = g$. Now by Lemma 4.3, we may write:

$$\mathcal{P}_2 f = \sum_{i \leq j}^{L} v_i (\mathcal{P}_1 \phi_i)(\mathcal{P}_1 \phi_j).$$

Finally, note that $\langle \cdot, \cdot \rangle_*$ obeys the inner product conditions of Lemma 4.5 on the range of $\mathcal{P}_2$, following from orthogonality and the normalization:

$$\langle \mathbf{p}_\alpha \mathbf{p}_\beta, \mathbf{p}_\alpha \mathbf{p}_\beta \rangle_* = \begin{cases} 2 & |\alpha| \neq |\beta| \\ 4 & |\alpha| = |\beta|, \quad \alpha \neq \beta \\ 8 & \alpha = \beta \end{cases}$$

So we can apply Lemma 4.5 to $\mathcal{P}_2 f, \mathcal{P}_2 g$, and the inner product $\langle \cdot, \cdot \rangle_*$. Hence, we can derive:

$$\min_{f \in \text{Sym}_L} \|f - g\|_{\mathcal{A}}^2 \overset{(a)}{\geq} \min_{f \in \text{Sym}_L} \|\mathcal{P}_2 f - \mathcal{P}_2 g\|_{\mathcal{A}}^2 \tag{4.140}$$

$$\overset{(b)}{\geq} \min_{f \in \text{Sym}_L} \|\mathcal{P}_2 f - \mathcal{P}_2 g\|_*^2 \tag{4.141}$$

$$\overset{(c)}{\geq} \min_{C,V} \frac{1}{2} \|C^T V C - 2 * \frac{1}{\sqrt{12T}} I\|_F^2 \tag{4.142}$$

$$= \min_{C,V} \frac{1}{6T} \|C^T V C - I\|_F^2 . \tag{4.143}$$

Here, (a) follows from the definition of $\mathcal{P}_2$ as an orthogonal projection with respect to $\langle \cdot, \cdot \rangle_{\mathcal{A}}$, (b) follows from the fact that $\| \cdot \|_{\mathcal{A}}^2 \geq \| \cdot \|_*^2$, and (c) follows from the application of Lemma 4.5. These matrices are elements of $\mathbb{C}^{T \times T}$, but the term $C^T V C$ is constrained to rank L. Hence, as before we calculate:

$$\min_{f \in \text{Sym}_L} \|f - g\|_{\mathcal{A}}^2 \geq \frac{T - L}{6T} = \frac{1}{6} - \frac{L}{6T} . \tag{4.144}$$

Letting $m = \min(N/2, D - 1)$ and assuming $m \geq 2$, it is a simple bound to calculate

$$T = \binom{N/2 + D - 1}{N/2} \geq \binom{2m}{m} \approx \frac{4^m}{\sqrt{\pi m}} \geq 2^m ,$$

and the bound follows.

□

This theorem demonstrates a hard function g that cannot be efficiently approximated by $f \in \text{Sym}_L$ for $L = \text{poly}(N, D)$, but it does not yet evince a separation. Indeed, observing that $\|g\|_\infty = \frac{1}{\sqrt{12T}} N^2 T = \frac{N^2 \sqrt{T}}{\sqrt{12}}$, g has very large magnitude, and there's no obvious way to easily approximate this function by an efficient network in Sym_L^2.

Thus, we consider a more complicated choice for g, that allows for the separation:

Theorem 4.16. *Let $D > 1$. Then let $g' = \frac{g}{\|g\|_{\mathcal{A}}}$ for g as defined in Lemma 4.11, such that $|g'\|_{\mathcal{A}} = 1$. Then for $L \leq N^{-2} \exp(O(D))$:*

$$\min_{f \in Sym_L} \|f - g'\|_{\mathcal{A}}^2 \geq \frac{1}{12} . \tag{4.145}$$

Proof. The lower bound follows almost identically as before. By Lemma 4.11.4 we still have that $\mathcal{P}_2 g' = g'$. So we can write

$$g = \sum_{1 \leq |\alpha| \leq N/2} g_\alpha \mathbf{P}_{\{\alpha,\alpha\}} \tag{4.146}$$

$$g' = \sum_{1 \leq |\alpha| \leq N/2} \frac{g_\alpha}{\|g\|_{\mathcal{A}}} \mathbf{P}_{\{\alpha,\alpha\}} . \tag{4.147}$$

Thus, by the same reasoning as Theorem 4.15 we recover the lower bound:

$$\min_{f \in Sym_L} \|f - g'\|_{\mathcal{A}}^2 \geq \min_{f \in Sym_L} \|\mathcal{P}_2 f - \mathcal{P}_2 g'\|_{\mathcal{A}}^2 \tag{4.148}$$

$$\geq \min_{f \in Sym_L} \|\mathcal{P}_2 f - \mathcal{P}_2 g'\|_*^2 \tag{4.149}$$

$$\geq \min_{C,V} \frac{1}{2} \|C^T V C - G'\|_F^2 , \tag{4.150}$$

where G' is the matrix induced by g' as given in Lemma 4.5, i.e. the diagonal matrix indexed by $G'_{\alpha\alpha} = \frac{2 g_\alpha}{\|g\|_{\mathcal{A}}}$.

Now, by the partial orthogonality of $\langle \cdot, \cdot \rangle_{\mathcal{A}}$ noted in Lemma 4.12, we have:

$$\|g\|_{\mathcal{A}}^2 = \sum_{1 \leq |\alpha| \leq N/2} \sum_{1 \leq |\beta| \leq N/2} \langle g_\alpha \mathbf{P}_{\{\alpha,\alpha\}}, g_\beta \mathbf{P}_{\{\beta,\beta\}} \rangle_{\mathcal{A}} \tag{4.151}$$

$$= \sum_{1 \leq |\alpha| \leq N/2} \sum_{1 \leq |\beta| \leq N/2} g_\alpha \overline{g_\beta} (12 \cdot \mathbb{1}_{\alpha=\beta}) \tag{4.152}$$

$$= 12 \sum_{1 \leq |\alpha| \leq N/2} |g_\alpha|^2 . \tag{4.153}$$

Hence, we can say

$$\|G'\|_F^2 = \sum_{1\leq|\alpha|\leq N/2} \left|\frac{2g_\alpha}{\|g\|_{\mathcal{A}}}\right|^2 \qquad (4.154)$$

$$= \frac{4\sum_{1\leq|\alpha|\leq N/2}|g_\alpha|^2}{12\sum_{1\leq|\alpha|\leq N/2}|g_\alpha|^2} \qquad (4.155)$$

$$= \frac{1}{3}. \qquad (4.156)$$

Call G'_L the best rank-L approximation of G' in the Frobenius norm. By classical properties of SVD it follows that G'_L is a diagonal matrix with L entries corresponding to the L largest elements of G'. Then because $\|G'\|_F^2 = \frac{1}{3}$:

$$\|G'_L - G'\|_F^2 = \frac{1}{3} - \sum_{l=1}^{L}\left(\frac{|2g_{\alpha_l}|}{\|g\|_{\mathcal{A}}}\right)^2, \qquad (4.157)$$

where we order $|g_{\alpha_l}|$ in non-increasing order.

Combining Lemma 4.11.2 and 4.11.4 yields the inequality that for all α such that $1 \leq |\alpha| \leq N/2$:

$$\left(\frac{|2g_\alpha|}{\|g\|_{\mathcal{A}}}\right)^2 \leq 4N^2\left(1-\left(\frac{1}{4}\right)^2\right)^{2D}, \qquad (4.158)$$

so we can conclude

$$\min_{f\in\text{Sym}_L}\|f-g'\|_{\mathcal{A}}^2 \geq \frac{1}{2}\|G'_L - G'\|_F^2 \qquad (4.159)$$

$$\geq \frac{1}{6} - 2LN^2\left(1-\left(\frac{1}{4}\right)^2\right)^{2D}. \qquad (4.160)$$

Hence, if $L \leq \frac{1}{24} \cdot N^{-2} \left(\frac{16}{15}\right)^{2D}$, we derive a lower bound:

$$\min_{f \in \text{Sym}_L} \|f - g'\|_{\mathcal{A}}^2 \geq \frac{1}{12}. \tag{4.161}$$

□

We remark here that in the instance $D > \sqrt{N/2}$, we replace D with $\hat{D}$ in the above bound, which is consistent with Theorem 4.8.

4.5 Proof of Upper Bound

In this section we prove the upper bound to representing g with an admissible activation that satisfies Assumption 4.7.

The strategy is as follows. In Section 4.5.1 we exactly encode the hard function g with an efficient network, but allowing the choice of very particular activation functions. In Section 4.5.2, we leverage Assumption 4.7 to build a network that approximates the exact one, using a given activation. We complete the proof in Section 4.5.3 by showing the exact and approximate networks stay close together, inducting through the layers.

4.5.1 Exact Representation

Let us first describe how to write g exactly with a network in Sym_L^2, using particular activations. We can then demonstrate to approximate those activations, which only introduces a polynomial dependence in the desired error bound ϵ.

For exact representation, the activations we will allow are $\xi \to \xi^2$, and $\xi \to \hat{\mu}_D(\xi)$. Note that from the fact that $\xi \cdot \omega = \frac{1}{2}\left((\xi + \omega)^2 - \xi^2 - \omega^2\right)$, we can exactly multiply scalars with these activations.

Then consider the following structure for $f \in \text{Sym}_L^2$ with $L = 1$. Given $x, x' \in \mathbb{C}^D$ with $|x_i| = |x_i'| = 1$ for all i, we define $\psi_1^*(x, x')$ via a network as follows. In particular, we will use $\cdot$ to explicitly indicate all scalar multiplication:

$$z^* = (x_1 \cdot x_1', \ldots, x_D \cdot x_D') \tag{4.162}$$

$$Z^{(1)*} = \left(\hat{\mu}_D(z_1^*), \ldots, \hat{\mu}_D(z_D^*)\right) \in \mathbb{C}^D \tag{4.163}$$

$$Z^{(2)*} = \left(Z_1^{(1)*} \cdot Z_2^{(1)*}, \ldots, Z_{D-1}^{(1)*} \cdot Z_D^{(1)*}\right) \in \mathbb{C}^{D/2} \tag{4.164}$$

$$\ldots \tag{4.165}$$

$$Z^{(\log_2 D)*} = Z_1^{(\log_2 D-1)*} \cdot Z_2^{(\log_2 D-1)*} \in \mathbb{C} \tag{4.166}$$

$$\psi_1^*(x, x') = Z^{(\log_2 D)*} \tag{4.167}$$

In other words, we exactly calculate $\psi_1^*(x, x') = h(x \circ x')$ through $\log_2 D$ layers by multiplying the terms $\hat{\mu}_D(z_i)$ at each layer. Note that $|z_i^*| = 1$ for all i. So by applying Lemma 4.9.3, it is the case that each entry $|Z_i^{(k)*}| = |\hat{\mu}_D(z_i^*)|^k \leq (1 + r^D)^D \leq 1 + 2^{-D}$ for all $k \leq \log_2 D$.

Now, for an input $\xi \in \mathbb{C}$ we define the map

$$\rho^*(\xi) = \frac{-4N^2 r^D + \xi}{\|g\|_{\mathcal{A}}}, \tag{4.168}$$

and it's easy to confirm that we exactly represent:

$$g'(X) = \rho^*\left(\sum_{n,n'=1}^{2N} \psi_1^*(x_n, x_n')\right). \tag{4.169}$$

4.5.2 Approximate Representation

Now, we can imitate the network above using the exp activation, and control the approximation error in the infinity norm. Let us assume we've chosen f_1, f_2 as in Assumption 4.7. Furthermore, let us define $\xi \star \omega = \frac{1}{2}(f_1(\xi + \omega) - f_1(\xi) - f_1(\omega))$, so that $\star$ approximates scalar multiplication.

Then we mimic the exact network via:

$$z = (x_1 \star x_1', \ldots, x_D \star x_D') \tag{4.170}$$

$$Z^{(1)} = (f_2(z_1), \ldots, f_2(z_D)) \in \mathbb{C}^D \tag{4.171}$$

$$Z^{(2)} = \left(Z_1^{(1)} \star Z_2^{(1)}, \ldots, Z_{D-1}^{(1)} \star Z_D^{(1)}\right) \in \mathbb{C}^{D/2} \tag{4.172}$$

$$\ldots \tag{4.173}$$

$$Z^{(\log_2 D)} = Z_1^{(\log_2 D-1)} \star Z_2^{(\log_2 D-1)} \in \mathbb{C} \tag{4.174}$$

$$\psi_1(x, x') = Z^{(\log_2 D)}. \tag{4.175}$$

In other words, we replace all instances of multiplication $\cdot$ with $\star$, and all instances of $\hat{\mu}_D$ with f_2. Finally, we define the map ρ as:

$$\rho(\xi) = \frac{4N^2}{\|g\|_{\mathcal{A}}} \cdot \left(\frac{\xi}{4N^2} \star 1 - r^D\right), \tag{4.176}$$

where we can clearly represent the constant r^D via one additional neuron.

4.5.3 Proof of Upper Bound

We complete the approximation of g' by showing the exact and approximate networks are nearly equivalent in infinity norm, leveraging the assumption on our activation.

Theorem 4.17. *Consider $\epsilon > 0$ such that $\epsilon \leq \min\left(\frac{1}{100}, \frac{1}{12D^2}\right)$. For $L = 1$, there exists $f \in \text{Sym}_L^2$, parameterized with an activation σ that satisfies Assumption 4.7, with width $O(D^3 + D^2 \log \frac{DN}{\epsilon})$, depth $O(\log D)$, and maximum weight magnitude $D \log D$ such that over inputs $X \in \mathbb{C}^{D \times 2N}$ with* unit norm entries:

$$\|f - g'\|_\infty \le \epsilon. \tag{4.177}$$

Proof. Let f be given by the Sym_L^2 network calculated in the previous section, i.e.

$$f(X) = \rho\left(\sum_{n,n'=1}^{2N} \psi_1(x_n, x'_{n'})\right). \tag{4.178}$$

Clearly $L = 1$. From Assumption 4.7 and what it guarantees about f_1 and f_2, it's clear that the maximum width of f is $O(D^3 + D^2 \log \frac{D}{\epsilon})$, the depth is $O(\log D)$, and the maximum weight magnitude is $O(D \log D)$.

We can prove the quality of approximation by matching layer by layer. First we note a quick lemma:

Lemma 4.18. *For $|\xi|, |\omega| \le \frac{3}{2}$:*

$$|\xi \star \omega - \xi \cdot \omega| \le \frac{3}{2}\epsilon. \tag{4.179}$$

Proof. Based on Assumption 4.7, note that for $|\xi|, |\omega| \le \frac{3}{2}$, we have that $|\xi + \omega| \le 3$ and therefore:

$$|\xi \star \omega - \xi \cdot \omega| \le \frac{1}{2}\left(|f_1(\xi + \omega) - (\xi + \omega)^2| + |f_1(\xi) - \xi^2| + |f_1(\omega) - \xi^2|\right) \tag{4.180}$$

$$\le \frac{3}{2}\epsilon. \tag{4.181}$$

□

It follows that, because all $|x_i| = 1$:

$$\|z^* - z\|_\infty = \max_{i \le D} |x_i \star x'_i - x_i \cdot x'_i| \le \frac{3}{2}\epsilon. \tag{4.182}$$

Now, because $|z_i^*| = 1$, it follows from our assumption on ϵ that $|z_i| \leq 1 + \frac{3}{2}\epsilon \leq 1 + \frac{1}{D}$. Hence, we can apply Lemma 4.9.6 and say

$$\|Z^{(1)*} - Z^{(1)}\|_\infty = \max_{i \leq D} |\hat{\mu}_D(z_i^*) - f_2(z_i)| \tag{4.183}$$

$$\leq \max_{i \leq D} |\hat{\mu}_D(z_i^*) - \hat{\mu}_D(z_i)| + |\hat{\mu}_D(z_i) - f_2(z_i)| \tag{4.184}$$

$$\overset{(a)}{\leq} 6\left(\frac{3}{2}\epsilon\right) - \epsilon \tag{4.185}$$

$$\leq 10\epsilon. \tag{4.186}$$

where (a) follows from Lemma 4.9.6 and Assumption 4.7 again.

Note, observe the following inequality, for any i:

$$|Z_{2i}^{(1)*} \cdot Z_{2i+1}^{(1)*} - Z_{2i}^{(1)} \cdot Z_{2i+1}^{(1)}| \leq |Z_{2i}^{(1)*} \cdot Z_{2i+1}^{(1)*} - Z_{2i}^{(1)*} \cdot Z_{2i+1}^{(1)}| + |Z_{2i}^{(1)*} \cdot Z_{2i+1}^{(1)} - Z_{2i}^{(1)} \cdot Z_{2i+1}^{(1)}| \tag{4.187}$$

$$= |Z_{2i}^{(1)*}| \cdot |Z_{2i+1}^{(1)*} - Z_{2i+1}^{(1)}| + |Z_{2i+1}^{(1)}| \cdot |Z_{2i}^{(1)*} - Z_{2i}^{(1)}| \tag{4.188}$$

$$= |\hat{\mu}_D(z_{2i}^*)| \cdot 10\epsilon + |f_2(z_{2i+1})| \cdot 10\epsilon \tag{4.189}$$

$$\overset{(a)}{\leq} 10\epsilon(|\hat{\mu}_D(z_{2i}^*)| - |\hat{\mu}_D(z_{2i+1})| + \epsilon) \tag{4.190}$$

$$\overset{(b)}{\leq} 10\epsilon\left(|\hat{\mu}_D(z_{2i}^*)| + |\hat{\mu}_D(z_{2i+1}^*)| + 6\left(\frac{3}{2}\epsilon\right) + \epsilon\right) \tag{4.191}$$

$$\overset{(c)}{\leq} 10\epsilon(1 + r^D + 1 + r^D + 4\epsilon + \epsilon) \tag{4.192}$$

$$\overset{(d)}{\leq} 10\epsilon(5/2) \tag{4.193}$$

$$\leq 25\epsilon, \tag{4.194}$$

where (a) follows from Assumption 4.7, (b) follows from Lemma 4.9.6, (c) follows from Lemma 4.9.3, and (d) follows from the fact that $\epsilon \leq \frac{1}{100}$.

Hence, to draw error bounds one layer higher, we calculate:

$$\|Z^{(2)*} - Z^{(2)}\|_\infty = \max_{i \leq D/2} |Z^{(1)*}_{2i} \cdot Z^{(1)*}_{2i+1} - Z^{(1)}_{2i} \star Z^{(1)}_{2i+1}| \tag{4.195}$$

$$\leq \max_{i \leq D/2} |Z^{(1)*}_{2i} \cdot Z^{(1)*}_{2i+1} - Z^{(1)}_{2i} \cdot Z^{(1)}_{2i+1}| + |Z^{(1)}_{2i} \cdot Z^{(1)}_{2i+1} - Z^{(1)}_{2i} \star Z^{(1)}_{2i+1}| \tag{4.196}$$

$$\overset{(a)}{\leq} 25\epsilon + \frac{3}{2}\epsilon \tag{4.197}$$

$$\leq 27\epsilon, \tag{4.198}$$

where in line (a) we apply Lemma 4.18 under the assumption that $|Z^{(1)}_i| \leq \frac{3}{2}$ for all i.

Note that from Lemma 4.9.3

$$|Z^{(1)}_i| \leq |Z^{(1)}_i - Z^{(1)*}_i| + |Z^{(1)*}_i| \tag{4.199}$$

$$\leq 10\epsilon + 1 + r^D < \frac{3}{2} \tag{4.200}$$

so this assumption is guaranteed.

We induct upwards through layers: assume that $\|Z^{(k)*} - Z^{(k)}\|_\infty \leq 3^{k+1}\epsilon$ for $k \geq 2$. Then:

$$|Z^{(k)*}_{2i} \cdot Z^{(k)*}_{2i+1} - Z^{(k)}_{2i} \cdot Z^{(k)}_{2i+1}| \leq |Z^{(k)*}_{2i} \cdot Z^{(k)*}_{2i+1} - Z^{(k)*}_{2i} \cdot Z^{(k)}_{2i+1}| + |Z^{(k)*}_{2i} \cdot Z^{(k)}_{2i+1} - Z^{(k)}_{2i} \cdot Z^{(k)}_{2i+1}| \tag{4.201}$$

$$= |Z^{(k)*}_{2i}| \cdot |Z^{(k)*}_{2i+1} - Z^{(k)}_{2i+1}| + |Z^{(k)}_{2i+1}| \cdot |Z^{(k)*}_{2i} - Z^{(k)}_{2i}| \tag{4.202}$$

$$\overset{(a)}{\leq} 3^{k+1}\epsilon(|Z^{(k)*}_{2i}| + |Z^{(k)}_{2i+1}|) \tag{4.203}$$

$$\overset{(b)}{\leq} 3^{k+1}\epsilon(|Z^{(k)*}_{2i}| + |Z^{(k)*}_{2i+1}| + 3^{k+1}\epsilon) \tag{4.204}$$

$$\overset{(c)}{\leq} 3^{k+1}\epsilon((1+r^D)^D + (1+r^D)^D + 3^{k+1}\epsilon) \tag{4.205}$$

$$\overset{(d)}{\leq} 3^{k+1}\epsilon\left(1 + 2^{-D} + 1 + 2^{-D} + \frac{1}{4}\right) \tag{4.206}$$

$$\leq 3^{k+1}\epsilon\left(\frac{11}{4}\right), \tag{4.207}$$

where (a) and (b) are both applications of the inductive hypothesis, (c) follows from Lemma

4.9.3, (d) is the binomial inequality and the fact that for any $k \leq \log_2 D$:

$$3^{k+1}\epsilon \leq 3\left(4^{\log_2 D}\right)\epsilon \tag{4.208}$$

$$= \frac{\epsilon}{3D^2} \tag{4.209}$$

$$\leq \frac{1}{4}. \tag{4.210}$$

And as before:

$$\|Z^{(k+1)*} - Z^{(k+1)}\|_\infty = \max_i |Z_{2i}^{(k)*} \cdot Z_{2i+1}^{(k)*} - Z_{2i}^{(k)} \star Z_{2i+1}^{(k)}| \tag{4.211}$$

$$\leq \max_i |Z_{2i}^{(k)*} \cdot Z_{2i+1}^{(k)*} - Z_{2i}^{(k)} \cdot Z_{2i+1}^{(k)}| + |Z_{2i}^{(k)} \cdot Z_{2i+1}^{(k)} - Z_{2i}^{(k)} \star Z_{2i+1}^{(k)}| \tag{4.212}$$

$$\overset{(a)}{\leq} 3^{k+1}\epsilon\left(\frac{11}{4}\right) + \frac{3}{2}\epsilon \tag{4.213}$$

$$\leq 3^{k+2}\epsilon, \tag{4.214}$$

where in line (a) we apply Lemma 4.18 under the assumption that $|Z_i^{(k)}| \leq \frac{3}{2}$ for all i.

Note that as before

$$|Z_i^{(k)}| \leq |Z_i^{(k)} - Z_i^{(k)*}| + |Z_i^{(k)*}| \tag{4.215}$$

$$\leq 3^{k+1}\epsilon + (1 + r^D)^D \tag{4.216}$$

$$\leq 3^{k+1}\epsilon + 1 + 2^{-D} \leq \frac{3}{2}, \tag{4.217}$$

so the assumption is granted.

Thus, completing the induction and remembering the definition of ψ_1, we conclude:

$$\|\psi_1^*(x_n, x_{n'}) - \psi_1(x_n, x_{r'})\|_\infty \leq 3^{\log_2 D + 1}\epsilon < 3D^2\epsilon. \tag{4.218}$$

Hence, we can finally bound the final networks:

$$\|g' - f\|_\infty = \left\|\rho^*\left(\sum_{n,n'=1}^{2N} \psi_1^*(x_n, x_{n'})\right) - \rho\left(\sum_{n,n'=1}^{2N} \psi_1(x_n, x_{n'})\right)\right\|_\infty \tag{4.219}$$

$$= \frac{1}{\|g\|_{\mathcal{A}}} \left\|\sum_{n,n'=1}^{2N} \psi_1^*(x_n, x_{n'}) - 4N^2\left(\left[\frac{1}{4N^2}\sum_{n,n'=1}^{2N} \psi_1(x_n, x_{n'})\right] \star 1\right)\right\|_\infty \tag{4.220}$$

$$\overset{(a)}{\leq} 4N^2 \left\|\frac{1}{4N^2}\sum_{n,n'=1}^{2N} \psi_1^*(x_n, x_{n'}) - \left(\left[\frac{1}{4N^2}\sum_{n,n'=1}^{2N} \psi_1(x_n, x_{n'})\right] \star 1\right)\right\|_\infty \tag{4.221}$$

$$\overset{(b)}{\leq} 4N^2 \left\|\frac{1}{4N^2}\sum_{n,n'=1}^{2N} \psi_1^*(x_n, x_{n'}) - \frac{1}{4N^2}\sum_{n,n'=1}^{2N} \psi_1^*(x_n, x_{n'})\right\|_\infty + 4N^2 \cdot \frac{3}{2}\epsilon \tag{4.222}$$

$$\leq 4N^2 \|\psi_1^*(x, x') - \psi(x, x')\|_\infty + 4N^2 \cdot \frac{3}{2}\epsilon \tag{4.223}$$

$$\leq 12N^2 D^2 \epsilon + 6N^2 \epsilon \tag{4.224}$$

$$\leq 18N^2 D^2 \epsilon, \tag{4.225}$$

where in (a) we apply the lower bound $\|g\|_A \geq 1$ from 4.11.2 and in (b) we once again apply Lemma 4.18, valid from the fact that for all X with unit norm entries:

$$\left|\frac{1}{4N^2}\sum_{n,n'=1}^{2N} \psi_1(x_n, x_{n'})\right| \leq 3D^2\epsilon \leq \frac{3}{2}. \tag{4.226}$$

So it remains to map $\epsilon \to \frac{\epsilon}{18N^2 D^2}$ in order to yield that $\|f - g'\| \leq \epsilon$. Note that this remapping only changes the maximum width to be $O(D^3 + D^2 \log \frac{ND}{\epsilon})$. $\square$

5 APPROXIMATING ANTISYMMETRIC FUNCTIONS WITH HIGH INTERACTION

In this chapter, we introduce a focus on networks that enforce *antisymmetry*, i.e. functions $\Psi : \mathbb{C}^N \to \mathbb{C}^N$ with the constraint:

$$\Psi(x_{\sigma(1)}, \ldots, x_{\sigma(N)}) = \text{sign}(\sigma)\Psi(x_1, \ldots, x_N) . \tag{5.1}$$

In other words, antisymmetric functions are similar to symmetric functions, but when the inputs are permuted, the sign of the function is flipped according to the sign of the corresponding permutation.

The antisymmetric constraint is an uncommon one, that primarily comes up in quantum chemistry. Specifically, it appears when solving Schröndinger's equation for quantum many-body systems, which is an eigenvalue problem of the form:

$$H\Psi = \lambda\Psi .$$

where H is some Hamiltonian operator, often based on a system of atomic nuclei and electrons.

Here one should consider N electrons that each occupy a spatial location in some input domain Ω, and Ψ the *wavefunction*, a complex-valued map $\Psi : \Omega^{\otimes N} \to \mathbb{C}$. The wavefunction completely characterizes the physical properties of the system: for example, the squared modulus

$|\Psi(x_1, \ldots, x_N)|^2$ gives the probability density of encountering the electrons in the spatial locations $(x_1, \ldots, x_N)$. A particularly important object is the *ground state*, which is the eigenfunction Ψ that is associated with the smallest eigenvalue of H. By definition, electrons are fermions, which means the wavefunction must satisfy the additional property of antisymmetry. Efforts to solve Schrödinger's equation directly by parameterizing the ground-state wavefunction must rely on an antisymmetric architecture [Pfau et al. 2020; Hermann et al. 2020], although we note there are alternative strategies [Carleo and Troyer 2017; Zhao et al. 2023].

In general, simple changes to the symmetric architectures like DeepSets typically don't suffice to enforce this new type of invariance, and therefore antisymmetry demands unique architectures. The focus of this work is on two of the simplest architectures that enforce antisymmetry. They are both characterized via the Slater determinant [Szabo and Ostlund 2012], which is the orthogonal projection of an arbitrary function over N inputs into the linear subspace of antisymmetric functions.

The first architecture, the *Slater ansatz*, models antisymmetric functions as a linear combination of several Slater determinants. This is akin to how a shallow, vanilla neural network is formed as a linear combination of simple non-linear ridge functions. This ansatz defines a universal approximation class for antisymmetric functions, but the approximation rates may be cursed by the dimensionality of the input space, as is the case when studying lower bounds for standard shallow neural networks [Maiorov and Meir 1998].

A more complicated architecture is the *Jastrow ansatz*, where each Slater determinant is 'augmented' with a symmetric prefactor [Jastrow 1955], which is to say multiplied by a permutation-invariant function. One can confirm that the product of an antisymmetric function with a symmetric one is again antisymmetric.

However, both these models are universal approximators, and there is no quantitative result that demonstrates the advantage of one model over the other via a particular hard antisymmetric function. Among practitioners, it is common knowledge that the Slater ansatz is inefficient for representing the ground state wavefunction Ψ for physically important electronic systems, compared to Jastrow. But a formal proof of this intuition, even for this setting when the electron domain Ω is one-dimensional, is absent from the literature. While advanced parameterizations such as backflow [Luo and Clark 2019], hidden fermions [Moreno et al. 2021], and Vandermonde-like parameterizations [Han et al. 2019a,b] are commonly used in practice, studying the simplest models is a crucial first step to understanding more elaborate models.

In terms of separating antisymmetric classes, [Huang et al. 2021] proves a non-constructive limit on the representability of the backflow ansatz, but requires exact representation rather than approximation in some norm. Conversely, [Hutter 2020] demonstrates the universality of a single backflow ansatz, but requires a highly discontinuous backflow transform that may not be efficiently representable with a neural network. Consequently, constructing an explicit antisymmetric function that realizes the separation is an open question, even in the seemingly simple setting of one-dimensional particles.

We are interested in understanding quantitative differences in approximation power between Slater and Jastrow. It turns out this question can be most easily addressed when the symmetric prefactor on G is a relational network [Santoro et al. 2017], and so the question mirrors the issue of depth separation based on set element interaction in Chapter 4. We prove the first explicit, quantitative separation between the two ansätze, and construct an antisymmetric function G^* that can be efficiently approximated with the Jastrow ansatz but requires exponential size to be approximated with the Slater ansatz.

5.1 Preliminaries

We consider N dimensional inputs, restricted to the complex unit circle. That is, $x \in \Omega^N$ with $\Omega = \{z \in \mathbb{C}; |z| = 1\}$. We denote the tensor product $\otimes$ where, for $f, g : \Omega \to \mathbb{C}$ we have $f \otimes g : \Omega^2 \to \mathbb{C}$ such that $(f \otimes g)(x, y) = f(x)g(y)$. Given a permutation $\sigma \in S_N$, and $x \in \Omega^N$, we denote by $\sigma.x = (x_{\sigma(1)}, \ldots, x_{\sigma(N)}) \in \Omega^N$ the natural group action.

Let $\mathcal{A}$ denote the antisymmetric projection operator, defined for rank-one functions and extended by linearity:

$$\mathcal{A}(f_1 \otimes \cdots \otimes f_N)(x) = \frac{1}{N!} \det \begin{bmatrix} f_1(x_1) & \cdots & f_1(x_N) \\ f_2(x_1) & \cdots & f_2(x_N) \\ & \cdots & \\ f_N(x_1) & \cdots & f_N(x_N) \end{bmatrix} \quad (5.2)$$

5.1.1 Antisymmetric Ansätze

We consider a Slater determinants as a term of the form $\mathcal{A}(f_1 \otimes \cdots \otimes f_N)$ (up to rescaling). Each f_n is referred to as an *orbital*. Thus the Slater determinant ansatz with L terms can be written as:

$$F = \sum_{l=1}^{L} \mathcal{A}(f_1^l \otimes \cdots \otimes f_N^l). \quad (5.3)$$

Similarly, the Jastrow ansatz (with only one term) [Jastrow 1955] can be written as:

$$G = p \cdot \mathcal{A}(g_1 \otimes \cdots \otimes g_N) \quad (5.4)$$

where p is a symmetric function, namely $p(\sigma.x) = p(x)$ for any σ and x. It is immediate to verify that G is antisymmetric.

Our primary goal in this work is to separate the Slater and Jastrow ansatz. But we make quick mention of the Backflow ansatz [Feynman and Cohen 1956] which can be defined as

$$\widetilde{G}(x) = \mathcal{A}(\tilde{g}_1 \otimes \ldots \tilde{g}_N)(\Phi(x)), \quad (5.5)$$

where $\Phi : \Omega^N \to \widetilde{\Omega}^N$ is an equivariant map, satisfying $\Phi(\sigma.x) = \sigma.\Phi(x)$.

Note that any Jastrow ansatz can be written in the form of a Backflow ansatz. Indeed, if

$$\Phi(x) = \begin{bmatrix} x_1 & \cdots & x_N \\ p(x)^{1/N} & \cdots & p(x)^{1/N} \end{bmatrix}$$

and $\tilde{g}_n(x_j, p) = g_n(x_j)p$, one can quickly verify that $G = \tilde{G}$. Therefore, quantitative separations between Slater and Jastrow automatically imply the same rates for Backflow.

5.1.2 Inner Products

To measure the distance between the Slater ansatz and the Jastrow ansatz, we need an appropriate norm. For univariate functions $f, g : S^1 \to \mathbb{C}$ we will use the S^1 inner product, in this chapter dropping the subscript:

$$\langle f, g \rangle := \langle f, g \rangle_{S^1} = \frac{1}{(2\pi)} \int_0^{2\pi} f(e^{i\theta}) \overline{g(e^{i\theta})} d\theta . \tag{5.6}$$

For functions acting on N particles, $F, G : (S^1)^N \to \mathbb{C}$, the associated inner product is

$$\langle F, G \rangle := \frac{1}{(2\pi)^N} \int_{[0,2\pi]^N} F(e^{i\theta}) \overline{G(e^{i\theta})} d\theta . \tag{5.7}$$

Observe that these inner products correspond to the input distribution where each electron is sampled uniformly iid from the complex unit circle. Then the orthogonality of the Fourier basis may be expressed in this notation by the fact that $\langle x^\alpha, x^\beta \rangle = \mathbb{1}_{\alpha = \beta}$.

5.1.3 Schur Polynomials

To construct relevant antisymmetric functions, we use several identities related to the symmetric Schur polynomials. First, we introduce some properties of partitions as they will be used to index Schur polynomials.

Partitions can be represented by their Young diagram, see Figure 5.1. Furthermore, we will

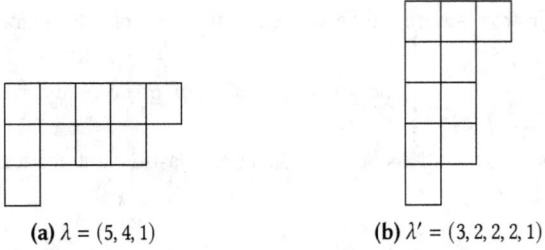

Figure 5.1: Example of Young diagram and conjugate partition

need the following notions:

Definition 5.1. Given a partition λ, the *conjugate partition* λ' is gotten by reflecting the Young diagram of λ along the line $y = -x$. We call a partition λ *even* if every part λ_i is even. Further, we call λ *doubly even* if λ and λ' are both even.

Reminding the Vandermonde written as:

$$V(x) = \prod_{i<j}(x_j - x_i). \tag{5.8}$$

Then we denote the Schur polynomial indexed by partition λ as:

$$s_\lambda(x) := \begin{cases} V(x)^{-1}\det\left[x_i^{\lambda_j+N-j}\right] & l(\lambda) \leq N, \\ 0 & l(\lambda) > N. \end{cases} \tag{5.9}$$

Given two partitions λ and μ, the following fact follows easily from linearity of the determinant:

$$\langle s_\lambda \cdot V, s_\mu \cdot V \rangle = N! \cdot \mathbb{1}_{\lambda=\mu}. \tag{5.10}$$

5.2 SEPARATION STATEMENT

Our main result is the characterization of a hard function G^*, such that the Slater ansatz F cannot approximate G^* without an exponential number of determinants (regardless of how the orbital functions are parameterized), while the Jastrow ansatz G can approximate G^* with a single determinant and efficient neural network parameterizations.

Theorem 5.2. *Consider a Slater ansatz with L terms:*

$$F = \sum_{l=1}^{L} \mathcal{A}(f_1^l \otimes \cdots \otimes f_N^l) \tag{5.11}$$

parameterized by orbitals $f_n^l : S^1 \to \mathbb{C}$, and a Jastrow ansatz

$$G = p \cdot \mathcal{A}(g_1 \otimes \cdots \otimes g_N) \tag{5.12}$$

parameterized by orbitals $g_n : S^1 \to \mathbb{C}$ and a symmetric Jastrow factor $p : (S^1)^N \to \mathbb{C}$.

Let $N \geq 6$ be even, and $1 > \epsilon > 0$. Then there is a hard antisymmetric function G^* with $\|G^*\| = 1$, such that G parameterized by a neural network with width, depth, and weights scaling in $O(\text{poly}(N, \log 1/\epsilon))$ can approximate G^*:

$$\|G - G^*\|_\infty < \epsilon \tag{5.13}$$

but, for a number of Slater determinants $L \leq e^{N^2}$:

$$\min_F \|F - G^*\|^2 \geq \frac{3}{10}. \tag{5.14}$$

The definition of G^* follows from the identity:

Theorem 5.3 ([Sundquist 1996] Theorem 5.2, [Ishikawa et al. 2006] Corollary 4.2).

$$\sum_{\lambda \text{ doubly even}} s_\lambda \cdot V = \text{Pf}\left[\frac{x_i - x_j}{1 - x_i^2 x_j^2}\right] \tag{5.15}$$

$$= \prod_{i<j} \frac{1}{1 - x_i^2 x_j^2} \cdot N! \cdot \mathcal{A}(\phi_1 \otimes \cdots \otimes \phi_N), \tag{5.16}$$

where we set the ϕ maps to be:

$$\phi_j(x_i) = \begin{cases} x_i(x_i^2)^{N/2-j}(1+x_i^4)^{j-1} & 1 \le j \le N/2 \\ (x_i^2)^{N-j}(1+x_i^4)^{j-1-N/2} & N/2+1 \le j \le N \end{cases} \tag{5.17}$$

For any $r \in \mathbb{R}$ with $|r| < 1$, by mapping $x \mapsto rx$ and using homogeneity of s_λ and V, we define G^* via the generating function identity:

$$G^* := \frac{C}{\sqrt{N!}} \sum_{\lambda \text{ doubly even}} r^{\left(|\lambda| + \frac{N(N-1)}{2}\right)} s_\lambda \cdot V = C\sqrt{N!} \cdot \prod_{i<j} \frac{1}{1 - r^4 x_i^2 x_j^2} \cdot \mathcal{A}(\phi_1^{(r)} \otimes \cdots \otimes \phi_N^{(r)}), \tag{5.18}$$

where

$$\phi_j^{(r)}(x_i) = \begin{cases} rx_i((rx_i)^2)^{N/2-j}(1+(rx_i)^4)^{j-1} & \text{if } 1 \le j \le N/2 \\ ((rx_i)^2)^{N-j}(1+(rx_i)^4)^{j-1-N/2} & \text{if } N/2+1 \le j \le N \end{cases} \tag{5.19}$$

where C is chosen to normalize G^*.

Note that from the RHS, it is clear that G^* is written in the form of a Jastrow ansatz. We will discuss efficiency of computing G^* in Lemma 5.9.

It remains to choose r and C such that $\|G^*\| = 1$. Note that, if $p(k)$ denotes the number of partitions of k, and and $p'(k)$ denotes the number of doubly even partitions of k, it's easy to see that

$$p'(k) = \begin{cases} p(k/4) & k \equiv 0 \mod 4 \\ 0 & \text{else} \end{cases} \tag{5.20}$$

So we calculate by orthogonality:

$$\|G^*\|^2 = \frac{C^2}{N!} \left(\sum_{\lambda \text{ doubly even}} r^{\left(|\lambda| + \frac{N(N-1)}{2}\right)} s_\lambda \cdot V, \sum_{\mu \text{ doubly even}} r^{\left(|\mu| + \frac{N(N-1)}{2}\right)} s_\mu \cdot V \right) \tag{5.21}$$

$$= C^2 r^{N(N-1)} \sum_{\lambda \text{ doubly even}} r^{2|\lambda|} \tag{5.22}$$

$$= C^2 r^{N(N-1)} \sum_{k=0}^{\infty} r^{2k} p'(k) \tag{5.23}$$

$$= C^2 r^{N(N-1)} \sum_{k=0}^{\infty} r^{8k} p(k) \tag{5.24}$$

$$= C^2 r^{N(N-1)} \prod_{k=1}^{\infty} \frac{1}{1 - r^{8k}} \tag{5.25}$$

where in the last line we employ the generating function for partition numbers. Then setting $C = \left(r^{-N(N-1)} \prod_{k=1}^{\infty} 1 - r^{8k} \right)^{1/2}$ gives $\|G^*\| = 1$.

Finally, we will choose $r = 1 - \frac{1}{\varepsilon N^4 + 8}$.

5.3 Proof of Lower Bound

We prove the lower bound of Theorem 5.2 by first bounding the Slater approximation in terms of the Frobenius norm of the corresponding flattened matrices, and then using SVD to control this bound.

5.3.1 Tensor Flattening

Definition 5.4. Let $\mathbb{N}_>^N$ denote the set of sequences of length N that are strictly decreasing non-negative integers. Introduce the index sets:

$$\mathfrak{A}_1 = \{\beta \in \mathbb{N}_>^{N/2} : \beta_i \equiv 1 \mod 2\} \tag{5.26}$$

$$\mathfrak{A}_2 = \{\gamma \in \mathbb{N}_>^{N/2} : \gamma_i \equiv 0 \mod 2\} \tag{5.27}$$

For $\beta \in \mathfrak{A}_1$ and $\gamma \in \mathfrak{A}_2$, let $\beta \cup \gamma \in \mathbb{N}^N$ be the concatenation of β and γ.

Then given a function F acting on N particles such as F, define the matrix $M(F)$ indexed by the sets $\mathfrak{A}_1$ and $\mathfrak{A}_2$:

$$M(F) = \left[\langle F, x^{\beta \cup \gamma}\rangle\right]_{\beta,\gamma} \tag{5.28}$$

Lemma 5.5. *For F as in Theorem 5.2:*

$$\|F - G^*\|^2 \geq N! \cdot \|M(F) - M(G^*)\|_F^2 \tag{5.29}$$

Proof. Note again that terms of the form x^α for $\alpha \in \mathbb{N}^N$ are orthonormal. Hence, we derive an initial lower bound by Bessel's inequality:

$$\|F - G^*\|^2 \geq \sum_{\alpha \in \mathbb{N}^N} (\langle F, x^\alpha\rangle - \langle G^*, x^\alpha\rangle)^2 . \tag{5.30}$$

Note that by antisymmetry of F and G^*, if α doesn't have distinct elements then

$$\langle F, x^\alpha\rangle = \langle G, x^\alpha\rangle = 0 . \tag{5.31}$$

To see this, suppose $\alpha_1 = \alpha_2$, and let P_{12} be the permutation operator defined by

$$P_{12}F(x_1, x_2, x_3, \ldots) = F(x_2, x_1, x_3, \ldots) \tag{5.32}$$

It's easy to see P_{12} is a symmetric operator with respect to $\langle \cdot, \cdot \rangle$. Then for any antisymmetric function H,

$$\langle H, x^\alpha \rangle = \langle H, P_{12} x^\alpha \rangle \tag{5.33}$$

$$= \langle P_{12} H, x^\alpha \rangle \tag{5.34}$$

$$= -\langle H, x^\alpha \rangle \tag{5.35}$$

which implies $\langle H, x^\alpha \rangle = 0$.

Furthermore, let us define the equivalence class $\sim$ as $\alpha \sim \alpha'$ iff there exists a permutation π such that $\alpha = \pi.\alpha'$. Then by similar reasoning, $\alpha \sim \alpha'$ implies:

$$\langle F, x^\alpha \rangle = (-1)^\pi \left\langle F, x^{\alpha'} \right\rangle \tag{5.36}$$

$$\langle G^*, x^\alpha \rangle = (-1)^\pi \left\langle G^*, x^{\alpha'} \right\rangle \tag{5.37}$$

From these facts, we can sum over all $N!$ permutations acting on an α with distinct parts, so we can write:

$$\|F - G^*\|^2 \geq N! \cdot \sum_{\alpha \in \mathbb{N}_>^N} (\langle F, x^\alpha \rangle - \langle G^*, x^\alpha \rangle)^2 \tag{5.38}$$

$$\geq N! \cdot \sum_{\beta \in \mathfrak{A}_1, \gamma \in \mathfrak{A}_2} \left(\left\langle F, x^{\beta \cup \gamma} \right\rangle - \left\langle G^*, x^{\beta \cup \gamma} \right\rangle \right)^2 \tag{5.39}$$

$$= N! \cdot \|M(F) - M(G^*)\|_F^2 \tag{5.40}$$

□

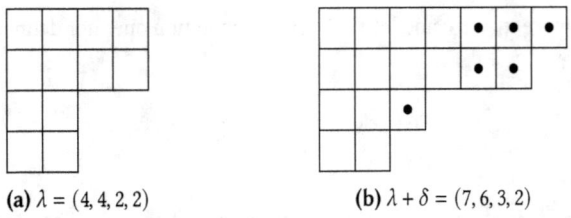

Figure 5.2: λ and $\lambda + \delta$ for λ doubly even.

5.3.2 Low-rank Approximation

Lemma 5.6. *Given F as in Theorem 5.2:*

$$N! \cdot \|M(F) - M(G^*)\|_F^2 \geq \frac{3}{10} \tag{5.41}$$

Proof. To begin, let us calculate the entries of these matrices. Let $\delta = (N-1, N-2, \ldots, 1, 0)$, and observe that:

$$\langle s_\lambda \cdot V, x^{\beta \cup \gamma} \rangle = \begin{cases} \pm 1 & \lambda + \delta \sim \beta \cup \gamma, \\ 0 & \text{otherwise.} \end{cases} \tag{5.42}$$

Note that ambiguity in sign depends on the sign of the permutation that maps $\lambda + \delta$ to $\beta \cup \gamma$.

By definition, G^* is a sum of terms of the form $s_\lambda \cdot V$ where λ is doubly even. This implies that $\lambda + \delta = (2a_1 + 1, 2a_1, 2a_2 + 1, 2a_2, \ldots)$ with $a_i > a_{i+1}$. In other words, $\lambda + \delta \sim (\gamma + 1) \cup \gamma$ with $\gamma + 1 \in \mathfrak{A}_1$ and $\gamma \in \mathfrak{A}_2$, where $\mathbf{1}$ is the all-ones vector. See Figure 5.2 for an example.

It follows that we may write:

$$\langle G^*, x^{\beta \cup \gamma} \rangle = \begin{cases} \pm \frac{C}{\sqrt{N!}} r^{\left(|\lambda| + \frac{N(N-1)}{2}\right)} & \beta = (\gamma + 1), \quad \lambda + \delta \sim (\gamma + 1) \cup \gamma, \\ 0 & \text{otherwise.} \end{cases} \tag{5.43}$$

Suppose we index $M(G^*)$ such that the ith column is indexed by $\gamma^{(i)}$, and the ith row is indexed by $\gamma^{(i)} + 1$. Then $M(G^*)$ is in fact a diagonal matrix. And given the functional form of G^*, we have that the diagonal terms will include:

- $\pm \frac{C}{\sqrt{N!}} r^{\left(0 + \frac{N(N-1)}{2}\right)}$ repeated $p(0)$ times,
- $\pm \frac{C}{\sqrt{N!}} r^{\left(4 + \frac{N(N-1)}{2}\right)}$ repeated $p(1)$ times,
- $\pm \frac{C}{\sqrt{N!}} r^{\left(8 + \frac{N(N-1)}{2}\right)}$ repeated $p(2)$ times,
- ...
- $\pm \frac{C}{\sqrt{N!}} r^{\left(4k + \frac{N(N-1)}{2}\right)}$ repeated $p(k)$ times.

Second, let us consider $M(f_1 \otimes \cdots \otimes f_N)$. We can calculate the inner product of a rank-one function as the product of orbital inner products:

$$\langle f_1 \otimes \cdots \otimes f_N, x^{\beta \cup \gamma} \rangle = \prod_{n=1}^{N/2} \langle f_n, x_n^{\beta_n} \rangle \prod_{n=1}^{N/2} \langle f_{N/2+n}, x_{N/2+n}^{\gamma_n} \rangle \tag{5.44}$$

Define vectors $u \in \mathbb{C}^{|\mathfrak{A}_1|}$ and $v \in \mathbb{C}^{|\mathfrak{A}_2|}$ such that

$$u_\beta = \prod_{n=1}^{N/2} \langle f_r, x_n^{\beta_n} \rangle, \tag{5.45}$$

$$v_\gamma = \prod_{n=1}^{N/2} \langle f_{N/2+n}, x_{N/2+n}^{\gamma_n} \rangle. \tag{5.46}$$

Then it's clear that $M(f_1 \otimes \cdots \otimes f_N) = uv^T$, i.e. it is rank-one. Consequently, because F is the sum of $L \cdot N!$ rank-one tensors, $M(F)$ will be rank at most $L \cdot N!$.

Thus, because $M(F)$ is low-rank and $M(G^*)$ is chosen to be diagonal, we have an approachable infinite-dimensional matrix low-rank approximation problem.

By SVD, the optimal choice for F is to produce a diagonal matrix $M(F)$ of rank $L \cdot N!$ with the maximal singular values of G^* along the diagonal. So it only remains to calculate these terms, and lower bound the approximation.

So suppose we choose $L \leq e^{N^2}$. Noting that $N^N \leq e^{N^2}/14$ for $N \geq 6$:

$$L \cdot N! \leq e^{N^2} N^N \tag{5.47}$$

$$\leq e^{2N^2}/14 \tag{5.48}$$

$$\leq p(N^4) \tag{5.49}$$

where the last line follows from Corollary 3.1 in [Maróti 2003].

So clearly $L \leq e^{N^2}$ guarantees that $L \cdot N! \leq \sum_{k=0}^{N^4} p(k)$.

Thus, since $M(F)$ is constrained to have rank $\leq L \cdot N!$, it will be diagonal with $\leq \sum_{k=0}^{N^4} p(k)$ terms, so that:

$$N! \cdot \|M(F) - M(G^*)\|_F^2 \geq N! \cdot \sum_{k=N^4+1}^{\infty} \left(\pm \frac{C}{\sqrt{N!}} r^{\left(4k + \frac{N(N-1)}{2}\right)} \right)^2 p(k) \tag{5.50}$$

$$= C^2 r^{N(N-1)} \sum_{k=N^4+1}^{\infty} r^{8k} p(k) \tag{5.51}$$

$$= 1 - C^2 r^{N(N-1)} \sum_{k=0}^{N^4} r^{8k} p(k) \tag{5.52}$$

where the last line follows as C was chosen so that $C^2 r^{N(N-1)} \sum_{k=0}^{\infty} r^{8k} p(k) = 1$.

Note that

$$\sum_{k=0}^{N^4} r^{8k} p(k) \leq \prod_{k=1}^{N^4} \frac{1}{1 - r^{8k}} \tag{5.53}$$

as the LHS is the generating function for partitions λ with $|\lambda| \leq N^4$, and the RHS is the generating function for partitions with all parts $\leq N^4$, which clearly dominates the LHS termwise.

So plugging back in the definition of $C = \left(r^{-N(N-1)} \prod_{k=1}^{\infty} 1 - r^{8k}\right)^{1/2}$:

$$N! \cdot \|M(F) - M(G^*)\|_F^2 \geq 1 - C^2 r^{N(N-1)} \prod_{k=1}^{N^4} \frac{1}{1 - r^{8k}} \tag{5.54}$$

$$= 1 - \prod_{k=N^4+1}^{\infty} 1 - r^{8k}. \tag{5.55}$$

Finally, remembering $r = 1 - \frac{1}{8N^4+8}$, we have:

$$1 - \prod_{k=N^4+1}^{\infty} 1 - r^{8k} \geq 1 - \left(1 - r^{8N^4+8}\right) \tag{5.56}$$

$$= \left(1 - \frac{1}{8N^4+8}\right)^{8N^4+8} \tag{5.57}$$

$$\geq \left(1 - \frac{1}{16}\right)^{16} \tag{5.58}$$

$$\geq \frac{3}{10}, \tag{5.59}$$

where we use that the limit $\left(1 - \frac{1}{n}\right)^n$ increases monotonically in n. □

5.4 Proof of Upper Bound

We prove the upper bound of Theorem 5.2 by directly approximating each component part of G^*, and the bound follows simply from the fact that G^* is already in the form of a Jastrow ansatz.

5.4.1 Approximation Lemmas

Observe first, the following well-known fact, essentially equivalent to the fact that the Discrete Fourier transform matrix is unitary:

Lemma 5.7. *Fix J and let γ be a primitive Jth root of unity. Then*

$$\frac{1}{J}\sum_{j=0}^{J-1} \gamma^{ij} = \begin{cases} 1 & i \equiv 0 \mod J \\ 0 & i \not\equiv 0 \mod J \end{cases} \quad (5.60)$$

From this fact and using an analytic activation function with sufficient decay, we can handily approximate any polynomial function on the complex unit circle with a polynomially-bounded shallow neural network.

Lemma 5.8. *For any $k, J \in \mathbb{N}$ with $4ek < J$, there exists a shallow neural network $f^{(k)}$ using either the* exp, sinh, sin *activations, with $O(J)$ neurons and $O(k)$ weights, such that*

$$\sup_{|\xi| \le 2} \left| f^{(k)}(\xi) - \xi^k \right| \le 2 \left(\frac{2ek}{J} \right)^J \quad (5.61)$$

$$(5.62)$$

The proof is straightforward, essentially using Lemma 5.7 to cancel all monomials not of the form ξ^t with $t \equiv k \mod N$, and using the quick decay to ignore all terms except ξ^k.

5.4.2 Jastrow Approximation

Lemma 5.9. *Let G and G^* be as in Theorem 5.2. Then for $\epsilon > 0$ and $N \ge 6$ even, there is a parameterization of G, with constant depth, where the total number of neurons and neuron weights are $poly(N, \log \frac{1}{\epsilon})$ such that*

$$\|G - G^*\|_\infty < \epsilon$$

Proof. We consider first the Jastrow factor of G^*. We will approximate it in G using a Relational Network [Santoro et al. 2017] with multiplication pooling. In what follows, we consider the infinity norm restricted to the unit complex circle.

Define $y_{ij} = f^{(2)}(x_i + x_j) - f^{(2)}(x_i) - f^{(2)}(x_j)$. Note that because $x_i x_j = (x_i + x_j)^2 - x_i^2 - x_j^2$, by Lemma 5.8, we have for an appropriate choice of J:

$$\|y_{ij} - x_i x_j\|_\infty \leq \|f^{(2)}(x_i + x_j) - (x_i + x_j)^2\|_\infty + \|f^{(2)}(x_i) - x_i^2\|_\infty + \|f^{(2)}(x_j) - x_j^2\|_\infty \quad (5.63)$$

$$\leq 6 \left(\frac{4e}{J}\right)^J \quad (5.64)$$

Clearly it follows that for sufficiently large J, $\|y_{ij}\|_\infty \leq 2$. Therefore, applying Lemma 5.8 again we have

$$\left\|f^{(2k)}(y_{ij}) - x_i^{2k} x_j^{2k}\right\|_\infty \leq \left\|f^{(2k)}(y_{ij}) - y_{ij}^{2k}\right\|_\infty + \left\|y_{ij}^{2k} - x_i^{2k} x_j^{2k}\right\|_\infty \quad (5.65)$$

$$\leq 2 \left(\frac{2ek}{J}\right)^J + \sum_{l=0}^{2k-1} \|y_{ij}^{2k-l}(x_i x_j)^l - y_{ij}^{2k-l-1}(x_i x_j)^{l+1}\|_\infty \quad (5.66)$$

$$\leq 2 \left(\frac{2ek}{J}\right)^J + \sum_{l=0}^{2k-1} \|y_{ij}^{2k-l-1}\|_\infty \|(x_i x_j)^l\|_\infty \|y_{ij} - x_i x_j\|_\infty \quad (5.67)$$

$$\leq 2 \left(\frac{2ek}{J}\right)^J + 2k \cdot 2^{2k} \cdot 6 \left(\frac{4k}{J}\right)^J \quad (5.68)$$

Now, consider a network g that takes in two inputs, defined via

$$g(x_i, x_j) = 1 + \sum_{k=1}^{K} r^{4k} f^{(2k)}\left(f^{(2)}(x_i + x_j) - f^{(2)}(x_i) - f^{(2)}(x_j)\right) \quad (5.69)$$

Then it follows that:

$$\left\|\frac{1}{1-r^4 x_i^2 x_j^2} - g(x_i, x_j)\right\|_\infty \leq \sum_{k=1}^{K} r^{4k} O\left(k 2^{2k} \left(\frac{2eK}{J}\right)^J\right) + \left\|\sum_{k=K+1}^{\infty} (r^4 x_i^2 x_j^2)^k\right\|_\infty \tag{5.70}$$

$$\leq O\left(K^2 2^{2K} \left(\frac{2eK}{J}\right)^J\right) + O\left(\frac{r^{4K}}{1-r}\right) =: \delta_1 \tag{5.71}$$

Let us assume we choose J, K such that $\delta_1 \leq 1$. One can confirm that

$$\max\left(\left\|\frac{1}{1-r^4 x_i^2 x_j^2}\right\|_\infty, \|g(x_i, x_j)\|_\infty\right) \leq \frac{1}{1-r} + \delta_1 \leq \frac{2}{1-r} \tag{5.72}$$

So it follows from routine calculation that

$$\left\|\prod_{i<j} \frac{1}{1-r^4 x_i^2 x_j^2} - \prod_{i<j} g(x_i, x_j)\right\|_\infty \leq N\left(\frac{2}{1-r}\right)^{N^2-1} \delta_1 \tag{5.73}$$

Consider second the antisymmetric factor. Following the row transforms given in the proof of Lemma 3.4 in [Ishikawa et al. 2006], the antisymmetric term may be equivalently written as:

$$\mathcal{A}(\phi_1^{(r)} \otimes \cdots \otimes \phi_N^{(r)}) = \mathcal{A}(\psi_1^{(r)} \otimes \cdots \otimes \psi_N^{(r)}) \tag{5.74}$$

with

$$\psi_j^{(r)}(x_i) = \begin{cases} rx_i((rx_i)^2)^{N/2-1} & j=1, \\ rx_i((rx_i)^2)^{N/2-j}(1+(rx_i)^{4(j-1)}) & 2 \leq j \leq N/2, \\ ((rx_i)^2)^{N/2-1} & j=N/2+1, \\ ((rx_i)^2)^{N-j}(1+(rx_i)^{4(j-1-N/2)}) & N/2+2 \leq j \leq N. \end{cases} \tag{5.75}$$

Expanding, we see that $\psi_j^{(r)}$ is a polynomial in degree $\leq 3N$ with only two non-zero coefficients, each bounded by 1. So by Lemma 5.8 it is easy to construct networks $\hat{\psi}_j$ such that

$$\|\psi_j^{(r)} - \hat{\psi}_j\|_\infty \leq \mathcal{O}\left(\left(\frac{6eN}{J}\right)^J\right) =: \delta_2 \qquad (5.76)$$

Choose J to ensure $\delta_2 \leq 1$, then we also clearly have that $\max\left(\|\hat{\psi}_j^{(r)}\|_\infty, \|\hat{\psi}_j\|_\infty\right) \leq 2 + \delta_2 \leq 3$. Now, we calculate:

$$\left\|\mathcal{A}(\psi_1^{(r)} \otimes \cdots \otimes \psi_N^{(r)}) - \mathcal{A}(\hat{\psi}_1 \otimes \cdots \otimes \hat{\psi}_N)\right\|_\infty \leq \frac{1}{N!}\sum_\sigma \left\|\left(\psi_{\sigma(1)}^{(r)} \otimes \cdots \otimes \psi_{\sigma(N)}^{(r)} - \hat{\psi}_{\sigma(1)} \otimes \cdots \otimes \hat{\psi}_{\sigma(N)}\right)\right\|_\infty$$

(5.77)

$$< N 3^{N-1} \delta_2 \qquad (5.78)$$

Finally, we combine the Jastrow factor and antisymmetric component. Let

$$G(x) = C\sqrt{N!} \prod_{i<j} g(x_i, x_j) \mathcal{A}(\hat{\psi}_1 \otimes \cdots \otimes \hat{\psi}_N)(x). \qquad (5.79)$$

Again, we have the simple bounds $\left\|\mathcal{A}(\psi_1^{(r)} \otimes \cdots \otimes \psi_N^{(r)})\right\|_\infty \leq 2^N$ and $\left\|\prod_{i<j} \frac{1}{1-r^4 x_i^2 x_j^2}\right\|_\infty \leq \left(\frac{2}{1-r}\right)^{N^2}$.

Then we calculate:

$$\|G^* - G\|_\infty = C\sqrt{N!} \left\| \prod_{i<j} \frac{1}{1-r^4 x_i^2 x_j^2} \cdot \mathcal{A}(\phi_1^{(r)} \otimes \cdots \otimes \phi_N^{(r)}) - \prod_{i<j} g(x_i, x_j) \cdot \mathcal{A}(\hat{\psi}_1 \otimes \cdots \otimes \hat{\psi}_N) \right\|_\infty \tag{5.80}$$

$$\leq C\sqrt{N!} \left(N 3^{N-1} \delta_2 \left(\frac{2}{1-r} \right)^{N^2} + N \left(\frac{2}{1-r} \right)^{N^2-1} \delta_1 2^N \right) \tag{5.81}$$

$$\leq \sqrt{N!} N 3^N \left(\frac{2}{1-r} \right)^{N^2} (\delta_1 + \delta_2) \tag{5.82}$$

From the choice $r = 1 - \frac{1}{8N^4+8}$ and the assumption that $N \geq 6$, we can further bound

$$\|G^* - G\|_\infty \leq N^{2N}(9N^4)^{N^2}(\delta_1 + \delta_2) \tag{5.83}$$

$$\leq N^{5N^2}(\delta_1 + \delta_2) \tag{5.84}$$

Choosing $J \geq 12eK$, and $K \geq 2$ so that $K^2 \leq 2^K$, we recall that

$$\delta_1 + \delta_2 \leq O\left(K^2 2^{2K} \left(\frac{6eK}{J} \right)^J \right) + O\left(\frac{r^{4K}}{1-r} \right) \tag{5.85}$$

$$\leq O\left(2^{3K-J} \right) + O\left(N^4 \left(1 - \frac{1}{N^4} \right)^{4K} \right) \tag{5.86}$$

$$\leq O\left(2^{-9K} \right) + O\left(N^4 e^{-4K/N^4} \right) \tag{5.87}$$

$$\leq O\left(N^4 e^{-4K/N^4} \right) \tag{5.88}$$

because the right-most term dominates in the second-to-last line.

Hence, if we'd like to control the error $\|G^*-G\|_\infty$ by some ϵ, we require that for some universal constant C,

$$\epsilon \geq CN^{\xi N^2+4} e^{-4K/N^4} \tag{5.89}$$

Note that for $N \geq 6$, we have $N^{5N^2+4} \leq e^{N^\xi}$, and therefore it suffices to choose K such that

$$\epsilon \geq C e^{N^3 - 4K/N^4} \tag{5.90}$$

And this condition is equivalent to the bound

$$K \geq \frac{1}{4}\left(N^4 \log \frac{C}{\epsilon} + N^7\right) \tag{5.91}$$

Note that J is subject to the same bound up to constant factors. □

6 | LEARNING A SINGLE SYMMETRIC NEURON

A popular model for studying SGD in non-convex settings is the single-index model, based on a student-teacher setup to provably learn a single neuron. Explicitly, the goal is to learn the function $x \mapsto f(\langle x, \theta^* \rangle)$ for some known map f and hidden direction $\theta^* \in \mathcal{S}_{d-1}$, trained with an identical architecture $x \mapsto f(\langle x, \theta \rangle)$ and an appropriate loss. This setting is an excellent testbed for two reasons: under a variety of assumptions, the non-convex optimization problem is nonetheless tractable to control convergence in gradient-based methods; and the explicit form of the true function means that generalization guarantees follow directly from accurate recovery of w^* and weak assumptions on the smoothness of f. Note that one could learn this model with a wide vanilla neural network that stays close to initialization [Chen et al. 2019; Nitanda et al. 2019; Ji et al. 2021], but this setting does not inform on the dynamics of feature learning as it doesn't exactly recover the hidden direction θ^*.

The conditions under which single-index model learning is possible have been well-explored in previous literature. The main assumptions that enable provably learning under gradient flow / gradient descent are monotonicity of the link function [Kakade et al. 2011; Kalai and Sastry 2009; Shalev-Shwartz et al. 2010; Yehudai and Shamir 2020] and Gaussian input distribution [Arous et al. 2021]. The first assumption essentially corresponds to the setting where the information exponent $s = 1$, as it will have positive correlation with a linear term. Under the second assumption, the optimal sample complexity was achieved in Damian et al. [2023], with study of learning when the link function is not known in Bietti et al. [2022].

When both assumptions are broken, the conditions on the input distribution of rotation invariance or approximate Gaussianity are nevertheless sufficient for learning guarantees [Bruna et al. 2023]. But more unusual distributions, especially in the complex domain that is most convenient for symmetric networks, are not well studied.

Adapting this setting to the case of DeepSets, we're essentially interested in the question if a student-teacher architecture can recover the simplest possible DeepSets model. As seen below, this will essentially correspond to a single-index setting where the inputs are first mapped through some symmetric feature extractor. But this prevents Gaussianity, and so without assuming monotonicity, we need a different way to analysis the loss of training a DeepSets architecture. Again, tricks from symmetric polynomial theory provide a way forward. We can analytically write down the loss of learning a single symmetric neuron, and for a judicious choice of the loss we obtain a complicated but ultimately tractable loss landscape. Hence, based on the information exponent of the link function f, we can with high probability recover the true hidden symmetric function through gradient flow in polynomial time.

6.1 Preliminaries

For $z \in \mathbb{C}$, we will use $\bar{z}$ to denote the complex conjugate, with the notation z^* always being reserved to denote a special value of z rather than an operation. For complex matrices A we will use $A^\dagger$ to denote the conjugate transpose. The standard inner product on $\mathbb{C}^N$ is written as $\langle \cdot, \cdot \rangle$, whereas inner products on $L^2(\gamma)$ spaces for some probability measure γ will be written as $\langle \cdot, \cdot \rangle_\gamma$. Furthermore, for h a vector and $p(x)$ a vector-valued function, we will use $\langle h, p \rangle_\gamma$ as shorthand for the notation $\langle h, p(\cdot) \rangle_\gamma$.

6.1.1 REGRESSION SETTING AND TEACHER FUNCTION

We consider a typical regression setting, where given samples $(x, y) \in \mathcal{X} \times \mathbb{C}$ with $y = F(x)$, we seek to learn a function F_w with parameter $w \in \mathbb{C}^M$ by minimizing some expected loss $\mathbb{E}_{x \sim \nu} [L(F(x), F_w(x))]$. Note that we consider complex-valued inputs and parameters because they greatly simplify the symmetric setting (see Proposition 6.2), hence we will also assume $\mathcal{X} \subseteq \mathbb{C}^N$. Both F and F_w will be permutation invariant functions, meaning that $F(x_{\pi(1)}, \ldots x_{\pi(N)}) = F(x_1, \ldots, x_N)$ for any permutation $\pi : \{1, N\} \to \{1, N\}$.

Typically the single index setting assumes that the trained architecture will exactly match the true architecture (e.g. as in [Arous et al. 2021]), but below we will see why it's necessary to consider slightly separate architectures. For that reason, we'll consider separately defining the teacher F and the student F_w.

Let $p(x) = [p_1(x), p_2(x), \ldots]$ be an infinite dimensional vector of powersums, and consider a fixed vector $h^* \in \mathbb{C}^\infty$ of unit norm. Then our teacher function F will be of the form

$$F : \mathcal{X} \to \mathbb{C} \tag{6.1}$$

$$x \mapsto F(x) := f(\langle h^*, p(x) \rangle) \tag{6.2}$$

for some scalar link function $f : \mathbb{C} \to \mathbb{C}$. F may thus be understood as a single-index function in the feature space of powersum polynomials. Note that this architecture can clearly be written in the form of DeepSets, by rewriting $\langle h^*, p(x) \rangle$ in the form $\sum_{n=1}^{N} \psi(x_n)$ for appropriate choice of ψ. In other words, the teacher is a DeepSets architecture with symmetric width $L = 1$.

6.1.2 DeepSets Student Function

Let us remind the typical structure of a DeepSets network [Zaheer et al. 2017], where for some maps $\Phi : \mathcal{X} \to \mathbb{C}^M$ and $\rho : \mathbb{C}^M \to \mathbb{C}$, the standard DeepSets architecture is of the form:

$$x \mapsto \rho\left(\phi_1(x), \ldots, \phi_M(x)\right). \tag{6.3}$$

where $\phi_m(x) = \sum_{n=1}^N \psi_m(x_n)$ for some map $\psi_m : \mathbb{C} \to \mathbb{C}$.

In order to parameterize our student network as a DeepSets model, we will make the simplest possible choices, while preserving its non-linear essence. To define our student network, we consider the symmetric embedding Φ as a one-layer neural network with no bias terms:

$$\phi_m(x) = \sum_{n=1}^N \sigma(a_m x_n), \tag{6.4}$$

for i.i.d. complex weights sampled uniformly from the complex circle $a_m \sim S^1$ and some activation $\sigma : \mathbb{C} \to \mathbb{C}$. And given some link function $g : \mathbb{C} \to \mathbb{C}$, we'll consider the mapping ρ as:

$$\rho_w(\cdot) = g(\langle w, \cdot \rangle), \tag{6.5}$$

where $w \in \mathbb{C}^M$ are our trainable weights. Putting all together, our student network thus becomes

$$F_w : \mathcal{X} \to \mathbb{C}$$

$$x \mapsto F_w(x) := g(\langle w, \Phi(x) \rangle). \tag{6.6}$$

In other words, F_w corresponds to a DeepSets network where the first and third layer weights are frozen, and only the second layer weights (with no biases) are trained.

The first fact we need is that, through simple algebra, the student may be rewritten in the form of a single-index model.

Proposition 6.1. *There is matrix $A \in \mathbb{C}^{\infty \times M}$ depending only the frozen weights $\{a_m\}_{m=1}^M$ and the activation $\sigma(z) = \sum_{k=1}^\infty c_k z^k$ such that*

$$g(\langle w, \Phi(x) \rangle) = g(\langle Aw, p(x) \rangle) \,. \tag{6.7}$$

where $A_{km} = c_k \sqrt{k} a_m^k$

6.1.3 Hermite-like Identity

In the vanilla single index setting, the key to giving an explicit expression for the expected loss (for Gaussian inputs) is a well-known identity of Hermite polynomials [O'Donnell 2021; Jacobsen 1996]. If h_k denotes the Hermite polynomial of degree k, this identity takes the form

$$\langle h_k(\langle \cdot, u \rangle), h_l(\langle \cdot, v \rangle) \rangle_{\gamma_n} = \delta_{kl} k! \langle u, v \rangle^k \,, \tag{6.8}$$

where $u, v \in \mathbb{R}^n$ and γ_n is the standard Gaussian distribution on n dimensions.

In our setting, as it turns out, one can establish an analogous identity, by considering a different input probability measure, and a bound on the degree of the link function. We will choose our input domain $\mathcal{X} = (S^1)^N$, and the input distribution we will consider is the squared Vandermonde density over N copies of the complex unit circle [Macdonald 1998].

Proposition 6.2. *Consider $h, \tilde{h} \in \mathbb{C}^\infty$ with bounded L_2 norm. For exponents k, l with $k \leq \sqrt{N}$, if h is only supported on the first $\sqrt{N}$ elements, then:*

$$\langle \langle h, p \rangle^k, \langle \tilde{h}, p \rangle^l \rangle_V = \delta_{kl} k! \langle h, \tilde{h} \rangle^k \,. \tag{6.9}$$

Proof. Based on the support assumptions and degree bounds, we can simply apply orthogonality of the powersums:

$$\langle\langle h,p\rangle^i, \langle \tilde{h}, p\rangle^j\rangle_V = \left\langle \sum_{|\alpha|=i} \binom{i}{\alpha} h^\alpha \overline{p^\alpha}, \sum_{|\alpha|=j} \binom{j}{\alpha} \tilde{h}^\alpha \overline{p^\alpha} \right\rangle_V \quad (6.10)$$

$$= \delta_{ij} \sum_{|\alpha|=i} \binom{i}{\alpha}^2 \langle p^\alpha, p^\alpha\rangle_V h^\alpha \overline{\tilde{h}^\alpha} \quad (6.11)$$

$$= \delta_{ij} \sum_{|\alpha|=i} \binom{i}{\alpha}^2 \left(\prod_{k=1}^{\sqrt{N}} \alpha_k!\right) h^\alpha \overline{\tilde{h}^\alpha} \quad (6.12)$$

$$= \delta_{ij} i! \sum_{|\alpha|=i} \binom{i}{\alpha} h^\alpha \overline{\tilde{h}^\alpha} \quad (6.13)$$

$$= \delta_{ij} i! \langle h, \tilde{h}\rangle^i \quad (6.14)$$

□

The crucial feature of this identity is that the assumptions on support and bounded degree only apply to $\langle h, p\rangle^k$, with no restrictions on the other term. In our learning problem, we can use this property to make these assumptions on the teacher function, while requiring no bounds on the terms of the student DeepSets architecture.

In order to take advantage of the assumptions on the support of h and the degree in the above proposition, we need to make the following assumptions on our teacher link function f and our true direction h^*:

Assumption 6.3. The link function f is analytic and only supported on the first $\sqrt{N}$ degree monomials, i.e.

$$f(z) = \sum_{j=1}^{\sqrt{N}} \frac{\alpha_j}{\sqrt{j!}} z^j \quad (6.15)$$

Furthermore, the vector h^* is only supported on the first $\sqrt{N}$ elements.

Although this assumption is required to apply the orthogonality property for our loss function in the following sections, we note that in principle, including exponentially small terms of higher degree in f or higher index in h^* should have negligible effect. Moreover, one should interpret this assumption as silently disappearing in the high-dimensional regime $N \to \infty$. For simplicity, we keep this assumption to make cleaner calculations and leave the issue of these small perturbations to future work.

6.1.4 Information Exponent

Because Proposition 6.2 takes inner products of monomials, it alludes to a very simple characterization of information exponent. Namely:

Definition 6.4. Consider an analytic function $f : \mathbb{C} \to \mathbb{C}$ that can be written in the form

$$f(z) = \sum_{j=0}^{\infty} \frac{\alpha_j}{\sqrt{j!}} z^j \tag{6.16}$$

Then the *information exponent* is defined as $s = \inf\{j \geq 1 : \alpha_j \neq 0\}$.

Similar to the Gaussian case [Arous et al. 2021; Bietti et al. 2022], the information exponent s will control the efficiency of learning. Assuming $|\alpha_s|$ is some non-negligible constant, the value of s will be far more important in governing the convergence rate.

6.2 Analytic Expression for Population Loss

In order to train the symmetric single index model, one must fix a loss. The L_2 loss of the typical single index setting is mathematically inconvenient, because the term $\|f(\langle Aw, p \rangle)\|_V^2$ lacks a closed form due to the high-degree terms. So we are driven to consider correlational loss functions, with regularization to control the landscape.

Let $\Re$ denote the real part, then a different choice of the loss might be:

$$\hat{L}(w) = -\Re E_{x \sim V}\left[f(\langle h^*, p(x)\rangle)\overline{\bar{f}(\langle Aw, p(x)\rangle)}\right] + \sum_{j=1}^{\sqrt{N}} \frac{|\alpha_j|^2}{2}\|Aw\|^{2j} \qquad (6.17)$$

$$= \sum_{j=1}^{\sqrt{N}} |\alpha_j|^2 \left(-r^j \cos j\theta + \frac{1}{2}(v+r^2)^j\right) \qquad (6.18)$$

where we apply Proposition 6.2 and introduce the variables $m = \langle Aw, h^*\rangle = re^{i\theta}$ and $v = \|Aw\|^2 - r^2$. Although this loss possess a global minima when $Aw = h^*$, i.e. when the student exactly recovers the hidden direction, this objective has a highly unfavorable landscape due to optimization of terms $\cos j\theta$, which corresponds to optimizing a non-trivial polynomial in $\cos \theta$.

Therefore, we consider a different choice of student link function that will enable a simpler analysis of the dynamics. For the choice of $g(z) = \frac{\alpha_s}{|\alpha_s|\sqrt{s!}} z^s$, we instead consider the loss

$$L(w) = -\Re E_{x \sim V}\left[f(\langle h^*, p(x)\rangle)\overline{g(\langle Aw, p(x)\rangle)}\right] + \frac{|\alpha_s|}{2}\|Aw\|^{2s} \qquad (6.19)$$

$$= -|\alpha_s|\Re\langle Aw, h^*\rangle^s + \frac{|\alpha_s|}{2}\|Aw\|^{2s}. \qquad (6.20)$$

where we simplify using Proposition 6.2. We note that Dudeja and Hsu [2018] used a similar trick of a correlational loss containing a single orthogonal polynomial in order to simplify the learning landscape. The global minima of this loss, and in fact the dynamics of gradient flow on it, will be explored in the sequel.

6.3 Derivation of Gradient Flow ODE

The gradient methods considered in Arous et al. [2021]; Ben Arous et al. [2022] are analyzed by reducing to a dimension-free dynamical system of the so-called summary statistics. For instance, in the vanilla single-index model, the summary statistics reduce to the scalar correlation between the learned weight and the true weight. In our case, we have three variables, owing to the fact that the correlation is complex and represented by two scalars, and a third variable controlling the norm of the weight since we aren't using projection. This considerably complicates the loss landscape, as even in gradient flow on the population loss the magnitude of the correlation $|\langle Aw, h^*\rangle|$ is not monotonically increasing towards one, but depends delicately on the state of the entire system.

Note that although our weight vector w is complex, we still apply regular gradient flow to the pair of weight vectors w_R, w_C where $w = w_R + iw_C$. Furthermore, we use the notation $\nabla := \nabla_w = \nabla_{w_R} + i\nabla_{w_C}$. With that in mind, we can summarize the dynamics of our gradient flow in the following Theorem.

Theorem 6.5. *Given a parameter w, consider the summary statistics $m = \langle Aw, h^*\rangle \in \mathbb{C}$ and $v = \|P_{h^*}^\perp Aw\|^2$ where $P_{h^*}^\perp$ is projection onto the orthogonal complement of h^*. Let the polar decomposition of m be $re^{i\theta}$.*

Then given the preconditioned gradient flow given by

$$\dot{w} = -\frac{1}{s|\alpha_s|}(A^\dagger A)^{-1}\nabla L(w), \tag{6.21}$$

the summary statistics obey the following system of ordinary differential equations:

$$\dot{r} = (1-\delta)r^{s-1}\cos s\theta - (v+r^2)^{s-1}r, \tag{6.22}$$

$$\frac{d}{dt}\cos s\theta = (1-\delta)sr^{s-2}(1-\cos^2 s\theta), \tag{6.23}$$

$$\dot{v} = 2\delta r^s \cos s\theta - 2(v+r^2)^{s-1}v, \tag{6.24}$$

where $\delta := 1 - \|P_A h^*\|^2$ and P_A is the projection onto the range of A.

Proof. We start from the analytic expression for the loss:

$$L(w) = -|\alpha_s|\Re\langle Aw, h^*\rangle^s + \frac{|\alpha_s|}{2}\|Aw\|^{2s} \tag{6.25}$$

To calculate the gradient with respect to the real and imaginary parts of w, we use tools from Wirtinger calculus [Fischer 2005]. Using the notation that $\nabla_{\overline{w}} = \frac{1}{2}(\nabla_{w_R} + i\nabla_{w_C})$ and the appropriate generalization of the chain rule, we have:

$$2\nabla_{\overline{w}}\Re\langle Aw, h^*\rangle^s = \nabla_{\overline{w}}\left(\langle Aw, h^*\rangle^s + \overline{\langle Aw, h^*\rangle^s}\right) \tag{6.26}$$

$$= \nabla_{\overline{w}}\overline{\langle Aw, h^*\rangle}^s \tag{6.27}$$

$$= s\overline{\langle Aw, h^*\rangle}^{s-1} A^\dagger h^* \tag{6.28}$$

Likewise,

$$2\nabla_{\overline{w}}\|Aw\|^{2s} = 2s\|Aw\|^{2(s-1)}\nabla_{\overline{w}}\|Aw\|^2 \tag{6.29}$$

$$= 2s\|Aw\|^{2(s-1)}\nabla_{\overline{w}}\left(w^\dagger A^\dagger Aw\right) \tag{6.30}$$

$$= 2s\|Aw\|^{2(s-1)}A^\dagger Aw \tag{6.31}$$

Thus, we have:

$$\nabla L = \nabla_{w_R} L + i\nabla_{w_C} L \tag{6.32}$$

$$= 2\nabla_{\overline{w}} L \tag{6.33}$$

$$= -s|\alpha_s|\overline{\langle Aw, h^*\rangle}^{s-1} A^\dagger h^* + s|\alpha_s|\|Aw\|^{2(s-1)}A^\dagger Aw \tag{6.34}$$

We introduce the parameters

$$m = \langle Aw, h^* \rangle = \langle w, A^\dagger h^* \rangle \tag{6.35}$$

$$v = \|P_{h^*}^\perp Aw\|^2 = \|Aw\|^2 - |m|^2 \tag{6.36}$$

And we consider preconditioned gradient flow of the form (where for complex variables we use similar notation that $\dot{w} = \dot{w}_R + \dot{w}_C i$):

$$\dot{w} = -\frac{1}{s|\alpha_s|}(A^\dagger A)^{-1} \nabla L \tag{6.37}$$

$$= \overline{m}^{s-1}(A^\dagger A)^{-1} A^\dagger h^* - \|Aw\|^{2(s-1)} w \tag{6.38}$$

It follows that

$$\dot{m} = \langle \dot{w}, A^\dagger h^* \rangle \tag{6.39}$$

$$= \|P_A h^*\|^2 \overline{m}^{s-1} - (v + |m|^2)^{s-1} m \tag{6.40}$$

where $P_A = A(A^\dagger A)^{-1} A^\dagger$ is the orthogonal projection onto the range of A. Let $m = a + bi = re^{i\theta}$, so we have $\dot{m} = \dot{a} + \dot{b}i$. Thus

$$\dot{a} = \|P_A h^*\|^2 r^{s-1} \cos(s-1)\theta - (v + r^2)^{s-1} r \cos\theta \tag{6.41}$$

$$\dot{b} = -\|P_A h^*\|^2 r^{s-1} \sin(s-1)\theta - (v + r^2)^{s-1} r \sin\theta \tag{6.42}$$

Now we do a change of variables, because $a = r\cos\theta$ and $b = r\sin\theta$, so

$$\dot{a} = \dot{r}\cos\theta - r\dot{\theta}\sin\theta \tag{6.43}$$

$$\dot{b} = \dot{r}\sin\theta + r\dot{\theta}\cos\theta \tag{6.44}$$

$$\tag{6.45}$$

Rearranging, we can get the flow on r and θ:

$$\dot{r} = \dot{a}\cos\theta + \dot{b}\sin\theta \tag{6.46}$$

$$= \|P_A h^*\|^2 r^{s-1}\cos s\theta - (v + r^2)^{s-1} r \tag{6.47}$$

$$r\dot{\theta} = -\dot{a}\sin\theta + \dot{b}\cos\theta \tag{6.48}$$

$$= -\|P_A h^*\|^2 r^{s-1}\sin s\theta \tag{6.49}$$

$$\tag{6.50}$$

We can instead control the flow on $\cos s\theta$:

$$\frac{d}{dt}\cos s\theta = -\dot{\theta}s\sin s\theta = \|P_A h^*\|^2 s r^{s-2}\sin^2 s\theta \tag{6.51}$$

and calculate the flow on v:

$$\dot{v} = 2\Re\langle A\dot{w}, Aw\rangle - 2r\dot{r} \tag{6.52}$$

$$= 2\left(r^s\cos s\theta - (v + r^2)^s - \|P_A h^*\|^2 r^s \cos s\theta + (v + r^2)^{s-1} r^2\right) \tag{6.53}$$

$$= 2(1 - \|P_A h^*\|^2) r^s \cos s\theta - 2(v + r^2)^{s-1} v \tag{6.54}$$

Finally, introducing the notation $\delta = 1 - \|P_A h^*\|^2$, we have

$$\dot{r} = (1-\delta)r^{s-1}\cos s\theta - (v+r^2)^{s-1}r \qquad (6.55)$$

$$\frac{d}{dt}\cos s\theta = (1-\delta)sr^{s-2}(1-\cos^2 s\theta) \qquad (6.56)$$

$$\dot{v} = 2\delta r^s \cos s\theta - 2(v+r^2)^{s-1}v \qquad (6.57)$$

$\square$

6.4 Bounding ODE Convergence

Given this form of the governing ODE, we can state conditions under which we approximately recover the hidden direction in polynomial time. First, we have a condition on the underlying activation function:

Assumption 6.6. We assume an analytic activation $\sigma(z) = \sum_{k=0}^{\infty} c_k z^k$, with the notation $\sigma_+ := \max_{1 \le k \le N} |c_k|\sqrt{k}$ and $\sigma_- := \min_{1 \le k \le \sqrt{N}} |c_k|\sqrt{k}$. We further assume:

(i) $c_k = 0$ iff $k = 0$,

(ii) σ analytic on the unit disk,

(iii) $1/\sigma_- = O(\text{poly}(N))$,

(iv) $\sum_{k=N+1}^{\infty} k|c_k|^2 \le e^{-O(\sqrt{N})}$.

These conditions essentially require that our analytic activation has non-negligible decay initially, that becomes more rapid later. As one example, it is quick to check that the function $\sigma(z) = \arctan \xi z + \xi z \arctan \xi z$ where $\xi = 1 - \frac{1}{\sqrt{N}}$ satisfies this condition.

Theorem 6.7 (Non-asymptotic Rates for Gradient Flow). *Suppose we initialize w from a standard complex Gaussian in dimension M with $M = O(N^3)$, and $\{a_m\}_{m=1}^M \sim S^1$ iid. Assume our activation satisfies Assumption 6.6. Furthermore, treat s and ϵ as constants relative to N. Then with probability $1/3 - 2\exp(-O(N))$, we will recover ϵ accuracy in all three sufficient statistics with time*

$$T \leq \begin{cases} O\left(\log \frac{1}{\epsilon}\right) & s = 1 \\ O\left(2^{s^2} N^{7s} + \log \frac{1}{\epsilon}\right) & s > 1. \end{cases} \quad (6.58)$$

To prove this result, we'll first show that the ODE reaches ϵ correctness with constant probability under certain initialization assumptions on the sufficient statistics, and then confirm that these assumptions are met under the weight initializations.

6.4.1 ODE Proof

Theorem 6.8. *Consider a fixed $\epsilon > 0$. Suppose the initialization of w_0 and $(a_m)_{m=1}^M$ are such that:*

(i) *Small correlation and anti-concentration at initialization: $0 < r_0 \leq 1$,*

(ii) *Initial phase condition: $\cos s\theta_0 \geq 1/2$,*

(iii) *Initial magnitude condition for Aw: $v_0 = 1 - r_0^2$,*

(iv) *Small Approximation of optimal error: $\delta \leq \min(\epsilon/2, O(s^{-s} r_0^4))$.*

Then if we run the gradient flow given in Theorem 6.5 we have ϵ accuracy in the sense that:

$$r_T \geq 1 - \epsilon, \quad \cos s\theta_T \geq 1 - \epsilon, \quad v_T \leq \epsilon \quad (6.59)$$

after time T, where depending on the information exponent s:

$$T \leq \begin{cases} O\left(\log \frac{1}{\epsilon}\right) & s = 1, \\ O\left(2^{s^2} r_0^{-4s} + \log \frac{1}{\epsilon}\right) & s > 1. \end{cases} \tag{6.60}$$

The following lemmas provide bounds on our dynamics that we can apply multiple times in different phases of the proof. Both of these lemmas are essentially special cases of the Bihari-LaSalle Inequality [Bihari 1956] stated for our setting.

Lemma 6.9. *Consider θ with the differential inequality*

$$\frac{d}{dt} \cos s\theta \geq k(1 - \cos^2 s\theta) \tag{6.61}$$

with $\cos s\theta_0 \geq 1/2$. Then we have

$$\cos s\theta_t \geq \tanh(kt) \tag{6.62}$$

and hence if $T = \inf\{t \geq 0 : \cos s\theta_t \geq c\}$, then $T \leq \frac{1}{2k} \log \frac{2}{1-c}$.

Lemma 6.10. *Consider $s \geq 2$. Suppose we have constants $0 < a < b$ and a function r of time t with differential identity:*

$$\dot{r} \geq ar^{s-1} - br^{2s-1} \tag{6.63}$$

Furthermore, assume $0 < r_0$ and it always the case that $r \leq 1$. Let $k = \frac{a}{b}$, and $T = \inf\{t \geq 0 : r \geq k^2\}$, then:

$$T \le \frac{1}{bk^2}\left(\frac{2E}{r_0^{s-1}} + \log\frac{1}{1-k}\right) \tag{6.64}$$

Proof of Theorem 6.8. We will use the following facts repeatedly in the below arguments.

First, because $\dot{r} \ge 0$ when $r = 0$, and $\dot{r} \le C$ when $r = 1$, it follows that r can never leave the range $[0, 1]$. Furthermore, note that $\cos s\theta$ is always non-decreasing.

6.4.2 CASE $s = 1$

In the setting with information complexity equal to 1, we immediately have the following identities:

$$\dot{r} = (1-\delta)\cos\theta - r \tag{6.65}$$

$$\frac{d}{dt}\cos\theta \ge (1-\delta)(1-\cos^2\theta) \tag{6.66}$$

$$\dot{v} \le 2\delta - 2v \tag{6.67}$$

Let us address v first. From our assumptions, $\delta < \epsilon$, and so when $v \ge \epsilon$, $\dot{v}$ is negative. It follows that a trajectory that begins below ϵ cannot ever exceed ϵ. In other words, if $v_0 \le \epsilon$, v can never exceed ϵ and we've achieved optimality.

Otherwise, supposing $v_0 > \epsilon$, consider values of t where $v_t > \delta$ so that the RHS of the inequality of $\dot{v}$ is strictly negative and we may write:

$$\frac{\dot{v}}{\delta - v} \ge 2 \tag{6.68}$$

Integrating from 0 to t gives that

$$-\log|\delta - v_t| - (-\log|\delta - v_0|) \geq 2t \qquad (6.69)$$

which yields the bound

$$v_t \leq \delta + (v_0 - \delta)e^{-2t} \leq \delta + e^{-2t} \qquad (6.70)$$

By Lemma 6.9,

$$\cos\theta_t \geq \tanh((1-\delta)t) \qquad (6.71)$$

Finally, we consider r.

Choose $T_1 = \inf\{t \geq 0 : v_t \leq \epsilon, \cos\theta_t \geq \frac{1-\epsilon/2}{1-\delta}\}$, and $T_2 = \inf\{t \geq T_1 : r_t \geq 1 - \epsilon\}$. Note that one can easily confirm that $T_1 \leq O\left(\log\frac{1}{\epsilon}\right)$

Then for all $t \in [T_1, T_2)$, we have

$$\dot{r}_t = (1-\delta)\cos\theta_t - r_t \geq 1 - \epsilon/2 - r_t \qquad (6.72)$$

and the RHS is always non-negative.

Dividing by the RHS and integrating from T_1 to t gives

$$-\log(1 - \epsilon/2 - r_t) + \log(1 - \epsilon/2 - r_{T_1}) \geq t - T_1 \tag{6.73}$$

Rearranging gives

$$r_t \geq 1 - \epsilon/2 - (1 - \epsilon/2 - r_{T_1})e^{T_1 - t} \tag{6.74}$$

Note that by definition of T_2, it follows that

$$1 - r_t \leq \epsilon/2 + e^{T_1 - t} \tag{6.75}$$

So it follows that $T_2 \leq T_1 + \log \frac{2}{\epsilon}$.

Altogether, the total time to achieve ϵ optimality for all three variables is $O\left(\log \frac{1}{\epsilon}\right)$.

6.4.3 Case $s > 1$

In this case, because we cannot straightforwardly solve or bound the system of ODEs, we need to control rates in stages. We have a stopping time for one variable at a time, and use local monotonicity to ensure bounds on the remaining variables.

FIRST PHASE In the first stage, we consider the duration of time $T_1 = \inf\{t \geq 0 : v_t \leq v^*\}$ where $v^* := 2^{-s}6^{-2}s^{-2}r_0^4$, and bound the behavior of each variable. Below, we will consider $t \in [0, T_1]$.

To control the behavior or r, we consider the following manipulations:

$$\frac{d}{dt}\log r^2 = 2(1-\delta)r^{s-2}\cos s\theta - 2(v+r^2)^{s-1} \tag{6.76}$$

$$\frac{d}{dt}\log v = 2\delta\frac{r^s \cos s\theta}{v} - 2(v+r^2)^{s-1} \tag{6.77}$$

This implies

$$\frac{d}{dt}\log\frac{r^2}{v} = 2r^{s-2}\cos s\theta\left(1-\delta-\delta\frac{r^2}{v}\right) \tag{6.78}$$

By definition, in this range of t we have $v_t > \frac{\delta}{1-\delta}$, so it follows that the RHS of this equation is always positive. Hence it follows that $\log\frac{r^2}{v}$ is increasing, and by monotonicity of log, we have

$$\frac{r^2}{v} \geq \frac{r_0^2}{v_0} \geq r_0^2 \tag{6.79}$$

This implies that

$$\dot r = (1-\delta)r^{s-1}\cos s\theta - (v+r^2)^{s-1}r \tag{6.80}$$

$$\geq (1-\delta)r^{s-1}\cos s\theta - \left(\frac{r^2}{r_0^2}+r^2\right)^{s-1}r \tag{6.81}$$

$$\geq r^{s-1}\left((1-\delta)\cos s\theta - \left(\frac{1}{r_0^2}+1\right)^{s-1}r^s\right) \tag{6.82}$$

Suppose it is true that $r \leq \frac{1}{6}r_0^2$, then it follows that:

$$r \leq \frac{r_0^2(1-\delta)\cos s\theta_0}{2} \tag{6.83}$$

$$\leq \frac{r_0^2(1-\delta)\cos s\theta_0}{r_0^2+1} \tag{6.84}$$

$$= \frac{(1-\delta)\cos s\theta_0}{\frac{1}{r_0^2}+1} \tag{6.85}$$

$$\leq \frac{((1-\delta)\cos s\theta)^{1/s}}{\left(\frac{1}{r_0^2}+1\right)^{\frac{s-1}{s}}} \tag{6.86}$$

So it follows that $\dot{r}$ will be positive whenever $r \leq \frac{1}{6}r_0^2$. We have $r_0 \geq \frac{1}{6}r_0^2$, it follows that $r_t \geq \frac{1}{6}r_0^2$ for $t \leq T_1$.

Finally we can control v by observing that, for $t \in [0, T_1]$, $v \geq v^* \geq (2\delta)^{1/s}$. Hence,

$$\dot{v} \leq 2\delta - 2v^s \leq -v^s \tag{6.87}$$

which implies

$$-\frac{\dot{v}}{v^s} \geq 1 \tag{6.88}$$

And integrating from 0 to $t \leq T_1$ gives

$$v_t^{-(s-1)} \geq \frac{1}{s-1}v_t^{-(s-1)} - \frac{1}{s-1}v_0^{-(s-1)} \geq t \tag{6.89}$$

Rearranging gives

$$v_t \leq t^{-\frac{1}{s-1}} \tag{6.90}$$

This gives a bound on $T_1 \leq (v^*)^{-(s-1)} = O(2^{s^2} r_0^{-4s})$.

Lastly by monotonicity we have $\cos s\theta_{T_1} \geq \cos s\theta_0$.

So to summarize:

$$r_{T_1} \geq \frac{1}{6} r_0^2 \tag{6.91}$$

$$\cos s\theta_{T_1} \geq \cos s\theta_0 \tag{6.92}$$

$$v_{T_1} \leq v^* \tag{6.93}$$

Furthermore, we've actually proven that $v_t \leq v^*$ for all $t \geq T_1$, which we will use in subsequent phases.

SECOND PHASE We define $T_2 = \inf\{t \geq T_1 : r_t \geq 1/5\}$. As before, if $r_{T_1} \geq 1/5$ then $T_2 = 0$ and we can skip to the next phase, so we assume otherwise.

Using the identity $(1+x)^k \leq 1 + 2^k x$ which holds for any $x \in [0,1]$ and $k \geq 1$, observe that the ODE governing r can now be bounded as:

$$\dot{r} = (1-\delta)\cos s\theta r^{s-1} - (v+r^2)^{s-1} r \tag{6.94}$$

$$\geq (1-\delta)\cos s\theta_0 r^{s-1} - \left(\frac{v}{r^2}+1\right)^{s-1} r^{2s-1} \tag{6.95}$$

$$\geq (1-\delta)\cos s\theta_0 r^{s-1} - \left(1 + 2^{s-1}\frac{v}{r^2}\right) r^{2s-1} \tag{6.96}$$

$$\geq \frac{1-\delta}{2} r^{s-1} - \left(1 + \frac{r_0^4}{2s^2(6r)^2}\right) r^{2s-1} \tag{6.97}$$

where in the last step we use that $v \leq v^*$ and plug in the definition of v^* and the bound $\cos s\theta_0 \geq 1/2$.

Consider any t when $r = \frac{1}{6}r_0^2$, and observe that the above inequality implies $\dot{r} > 0$. Because $r_{T_1} \geq \frac{1}{6}r_0^2$, this implies we will always have $r \geq \frac{1}{6}r_0^2$ for larger values of t, and we may bound:

$$\dot{r} \geq \frac{1-\delta}{2}r^{s-1} - \left(1 + \frac{1}{2s^2}\right)r^{2s-1} \tag{6.98}$$

Hence, we can apply Lemma 6.10 with $a = (1-\delta)/2$, $b = 1 + \frac{1}{2s^2}$, where $k^2 = (a/b)^2 \geq 1/5$, and using the initialization of r_{T_1}. This grants the bound that $T_2 \leq T_1 + O(s^4 r_{T_1}^{-s+1}) = T_1 + O(6^s r_0^{-2s+2})$.

Therefore the new summary is:

$$r_{T_2} \geq 1/5 \tag{6.99}$$

$$\cos s\theta_{T_2} \geq \cos s\theta_0 \tag{6.100}$$

$$v_{T_2} \leq v^* \tag{6.101}$$

THIRD PHASE We define $T_3 = \inf\{t \geq T_2 : \cos s\theta_t \geq \frac{1 - \frac{1}{4s^4}}{1 - \delta}\}$

First of all, note that the bound on r derived in the last phase required lower bounding $\cos s\theta$ by $\cos s\theta_0$. Since $\cos s\theta$ is non-decreasing, that bound is still true by an identical argument. So we can bound the ODE for θ:

$$\frac{d}{dt}\cos s\theta = (1-\delta)sr^{s-2}(1 - \cos^2 s\theta) \tag{6.102}$$

$$\geq (1-\delta)s(1/5)^{s-2}(1 - \cos^2 s\theta) \tag{6.103}$$

121

Note that by lemma 6.9 with $k = (1-\delta)s(1/5)^{s-2}$, we have

$$T_3 \leq T_2 + O(5^s \log s) \tag{6.104}$$

The bound $v \leq v^*$ continues to hold. In summary, we now have:

$$r_{T_3} \geq 1/5 \tag{6.105}$$

$$\cos s\theta_{T_3} \geq \frac{1 - \frac{1}{4s^4}}{1-\delta} \tag{6.106}$$

$$v_{T_3} \leq v^* \tag{6.107}$$

FOURTH PHASE We define $T_4 = \inf\{t \geq T_3 : r_t \geq r^*\}$ where $r^* := 1 - \frac{1}{s^2}$. Again, consider the non-trivial case where $T_4 \neq 0$.

Because the bound on v is the same, and the bound on $\cos s\theta$ is better than before, we can now bound the ODE of r similarly to the second phase:

$$\dot{r} \geq \left(1 - \frac{1}{4s^4}\right) r^{s-1} - \left(1 + \frac{1}{2s^2}\right) r^{2s-1} \tag{6.108}$$

Applying Lemma 6.10 with $k = \frac{1 - \frac{1}{4s^4}}{1 + \frac{1}{2s^2}} = 1 - \frac{1}{2s^2}$, we have:

$$T = \inf\{t \geq T_3 : r \geq k^2\} \leq T_3 + O(5^s \log s) \tag{6.109}$$

Finally, note that $k^2 = \left(1 - \frac{1}{2s^2}\right)^2 \geq 1 - \frac{1}{s^2}$, which implies that $T_4 \leq T$.

Thus we have:

$$r_{T_4} \geq r^* \tag{6.110}$$

$$\cos s\theta_{T_4} \geq \frac{1 - \frac{1}{4s^4}}{1 - \delta} \tag{6.111}$$

$$v_{T_4} \leq v^* \tag{6.112}$$

FIFTH PHASE   We define $T_5 = \inf\{t \geq T_4 : \cos s\theta_t \geq \frac{1-\epsilon/2}{1-\delta}, v_t \leq v^\dagger\}$ where $v^\dagger = 2^{-s}(\epsilon/2)(r^*)^2$.

Again, since $\cos s\theta$ is increasing and v is always less than v^*, the bound on $r \geq r^*$ established in the last step will stay true.

Thus, by the identity $r^k \geq (r^*)^k = \left(1 - \frac{1}{s^2}\right)^k \geq 1 - \frac{k}{s^2}$ we have the ODE inequalities:

$$\frac{d}{dt}\cos s\theta = (1 - \delta)sr^{s-2}(1 - \cos^2 s\theta) \tag{6.113}$$

$$\geq (1 - \mathcal{E})s\left(1 - \frac{1}{s}\right)(1 - \cos^2 s\theta) \tag{6.114}$$

$$\dot{v} = 2\delta r^s \cos s\theta - 2(v + r^2)^{s-1}v \tag{6.115}$$

$$\leq 2\delta - \varepsilon\left(1 - \frac{2(s-1)}{s^2}\right)v \tag{6.116}$$

It is easy to see that we'll have the bound

$$T_5 \leq T_4 + O\left(\log\frac{1}{\epsilon}\right) \tag{6.117}$$

and in summary

$$r_{T_5} \geq r^* \tag{6.118}$$

$$\cos s\theta_{T_5} \geq \frac{1-\epsilon/2}{1-\delta} \tag{6.119}$$

$$v_{T_5} \leq v^\dagger \tag{6.120}$$

SIXTH PHASE We define $T_6 = \inf\{t \geq T_5 : r_t \geq 1-\epsilon\}$, and assume the non-trivial setting where $T_6 \neq 0$.

Note that $\dot{v}$ is negative when $v = v^\dagger$, so the bound $v \leq v^\dagger$ remains true for $t \geq T_5$. Thus, we can control the ODE of r one more time:

$$\dot{r} = (1-\delta)r^{s-1}\cos s\theta - (v+r^2)^{s-1}r \tag{6.121}$$

$$\geq (1-\delta)r^{s-1}(1-\epsilon/2) - \left(1+\frac{v}{r^2}\right)^{s-1}r \tag{6.122}$$

$$\geq (1-\epsilon/2)r^{s-1} - \left(1+2^s\frac{v^\dagger}{r^2}\right)r^{2s-1} \tag{6.123}$$

$$\geq (1-\epsilon/2)r^{s-1} - \left(1+\epsilon/2\frac{(r^*)^2}{r^2}\right)r^{2s-1} \tag{6.124}$$

One can confirm that when $r = r^*$, the RHS of the above inequality is positive, so $\dot{r} \geq 0$. Thus, since $r_{T_5} \geq r^*$, it will always be the case that $r \geq r^*$ for $t \geq T_5$, so as before we bound:

$$\dot{r} \geq (1-\epsilon/2)r^{s-1} - (1+\epsilon/2)r^{2s-1} \tag{6.125}$$

By Lemma 6.10, we have that

$$T_6 \leq T_5 + O\left(\log \frac{1}{\epsilon}\right) \tag{6.126}$$

and thus we've achieved ϵ optimality for all three of our variables. □

6.4.4 Concentration Lemmas

We need two standard concentration inequality results. Both these results are special cases of more general results stated in [Vershynin 2018] for real-valued subgaussian variables, but it's standard to extend them to complex-valued random variables with appropriate tail bounds:

Lemma 6.11 (Theorem 3.1.1 in Vershynin [2018]). *If w is drawn from the standard complex Gaussian on M dimensions, then*

$$P(|\|w\| - \sqrt{M}| \geq t) \leq 2\exp(-ct^2) \tag{6.127}$$

for some universal constant c.

Lemma 6.12 (Theorem 4.6.1 from Vershynin [2018]). *Let $a_m \sim S^1$ be sampled iid, for $m = 1, \ldots, M$, and define $X \in \mathbb{C}^{N \times M}$ as $X_{nm} = a_m^n$. Then if we choose $M = O(N^3)$, with probability $1 - 2\exp(-O(N))$:*

$$\sigma_1(X) = \Theta(\sqrt{M}), \sigma_N(X) = \Theta(\sqrt{M}) \tag{6.128}$$

6.4.5 Projection Proof

The first two conditions of Theorem 6.8 are simply required for the application of Proposition 6.2, as the powersum vector p is built out of polynomials induced by the activation and does not include a constant term. The second two conditions concern the decay of the coefficients of σ, in the sense that the decay must start slow but eventually become very rapid. These conditions are necessary mainly for ensuring the Small Approximation of optimal error condition:

Lemma 6.13. *Let σ satisfy Assumption 6.6, and assume $M = O(N^3)$. Then for any unit norm $h^* \in \mathbb{C}^\infty$ that is only supported on the first $\sqrt{N}$ elements, with probability $1 - 2\exp(-O(N))$:*

$$1 - \|P_A h^*\|^2 \leq e^{-O(\sqrt{N})}.$$

Proof. Remind from Proposition 6.1 that $A \in \mathbb{C}^{\infty \times M}$ is of the form

$$A_{km} = c_k \sqrt{k} a_m^k \tag{6.129}$$

where we assume $c_k > 0$, and $a_m \sim S^1$. Note that

$$1 - \|P_A h^*\|^2 = \|P_A^\perp h^*\|^2 \tag{6.130}$$

$$= \min_w \|Aw - h^*\|^2 \tag{6.131}$$

$$\tag{6.132}$$

so we need to choose a candidate value of w.

Consider the block decomposition

$$A = \left[\begin{array}{c} B \\ \hline C \end{array}\right] \tag{6.133}$$

where $B \in \mathbb{C}^{N \times M}$ and $C \in \mathbb{C}^{\infty \times M}$. Suppose we decompose $h^* = \left[\begin{array}{c} u \\ \hline 0 \end{array}\right]$ where $u \in \mathbb{C}^N$. Then if we apply the pseudoinverse and define $w = B^+ u$, observe:

$$Aw = \left[\begin{array}{c} B \\ \hline C \end{array}\right] B^+ u \tag{6.134}$$

$$= \left[\begin{array}{c} BB^+ u \\ \hline CB^+ u \end{array}\right] \tag{6.135}$$

Observe that we can decompose $B = DX$ where D is a diagonal matrix such that $D_{kk} = c_k \sqrt{k}$ and $X_{km} = a_m^k$. Since $N < M$, one can see X is a rectangular Vandermonde matrix evaluated on $\{a_m\}_{m=1}^M$. Almost surely, these values are all pairwise distinct, which implies that X has linearly independent rows. Since D is diagonal with no zeros along the diagonal, B also has linearly independent rows. This condition implies $BB^+ = I$. So we have

$$Aw = \left[\begin{array}{c} u \\ \hline CB^+ u \end{array}\right] \tag{6.136}$$

Remember $\|u\| = \|h^*\| = 1$, as u is the first N elements of h^* and hence still only supported on the first $\sqrt{N}$ elements. Because $B^+ = X^+ D^{-1}$ we have:

$$\|CB^+ u\| \leq \|C\|\|X^+\|\|D^{-1}u\| \tag{6.137}$$

$$\tag{6.138}$$

We can now go about bounding these norms.

Since u is only supported on the first $\sqrt{N}$ elements and $\|u\| = 1$, it follows $\|D^{-1}u\| \leq \max_{1 \leq k \leq \sqrt{N}} \left|\frac{1}{c_k \sqrt{k}}\right| = \frac{1}{\sigma_-}$.

By Lemma 6.12, we have the bound

$$\|X^+\| \leq O\left(\frac{1}{\sqrt{M}}\right) \tag{6.139}$$

Finally for any $\hat{w} \in \mathbb{C}^M$ with $\|\hat{w}\| = 1$, we have by Cauchy-Schwarz:

$$\|Cw\|^2 = \sum_{k=N+1}^{\infty} \left|\sum_{m=1}^{M} \hat{w}_m c_k \sqrt{k} a_m^k\right|^2 \tag{6.140}$$

$$\leq \sum_{k=N+1}^{\infty} \|\hat{w}\|^2 \sum_{m=1}^{M} \left|c_k \sqrt{k}\right|^2 \tag{6.141}$$

$$= M \sum_{k=N+1}^{\infty} k|c_k|^2 \tag{6.142}$$

$$\leq M e^{-O(\sqrt{N})} \tag{6.143}$$

where we use in the last step Assumption 6.6.

With these bounds, we clearly have

$$1 - |P_A h^*| \le |Aw - h^*|^2 \tag{6.144}$$

$$= \left\| \begin{bmatrix} u \\ CB^+u \end{bmatrix} - \begin{bmatrix} u \\ 0 \end{bmatrix} \right\|^2 \tag{6.145}$$

$$\le |CB^+u|^2 \tag{6.146}$$

$$\le \frac{M}{\sqrt{M}\sigma_-} e^{-O(\sqrt{N})} \tag{6.147}$$

Because $M = O(N^3)$, and we've assumed $1/\sigma_-$ is polynomial in N, this bound can be written as $e^{-O(\sqrt{N})}$ for possibly different constants in the big O notation.

□

6.4.6 Initialization Proof

Lastly, we can choose an initialization scheme for w which handily ensures the remaining assumptions we need to apply Theorem 6.8. The crucial features of σ are similar to the previous result. Namely, we want the initial correlation r_0 to be non-negligible because this directly controls the runtime of gradient flow. Slow initial decay with fast late decay of the σ coefficients directly implies that Aw_0 has a lot of mass in the first $\sqrt{N}$ indices and very little mass past the first N indices. These requirements rule out, say, exp as an analytic activation because the coefficients decay too rapidly.

Lemma 6.14. *Suppose w is sampled from a standard complex Gaussian on M variables. It follows that if we set $w_0 = \frac{w}{\|Aw\|}$, and use the summary statistics from Theorem 6.5, then with probability $1/3 - 2\exp(-O(N))$ and any h^* as in Lemma 6.13*

(i) $1 \ge r_0 \ge c\frac{\sigma_-}{\sigma_+\sqrt{M}}$ *for some universal constant $c > 0$,*

(ii) $\cos s\theta_0 \ge 1/2$,

(iii) $v_0 = 1 - r_0^2$.

Proof. Remind that $m_0 = \langle Aw_0, h^* \rangle = \frac{1}{\|Aw\|}\langle Aw, h^* \rangle$. Because the complex Gaussian is invariant to multiplication by an unit modulus complex number, it follows that θ_0 is independent of r_0 and uniformly distributed on S^1. Because s is a positive integer, $s\theta_0$ is also uniformly distributed on S^1, and hence $P(\cos s\theta_0 \geq 1/2) = 1/3$. And by our choice of normalization, $v_0 = 1 - r_0^2$ automatically. So it only remains to prove the first statement is true with high probability.

We remind that $r_0 = \frac{|\langle Aw, h^* \rangle|}{\|Aw\|}$. By Cauchy-Schwartz, it's clear that $r_0 \leq 1$, so only the lower bound is non-trivial. If we use the same notation to decompose the matrix A as in the proof of Lemma 6.13, it's clear that

$$|\langle Aw, h^* \rangle| = |\langle Bw, u \rangle| \tag{6.148}$$
$$= |\langle w, B^\dagger u \rangle| \tag{6.149}$$

If we condition on B, then by rotation invariance of the Gaussian, note that $|\langle w, B^\dagger u \rangle|$ is distributed identically to $|g|\|B^\dagger u\|$ where g is sampled from a one dimensional complex Gaussian. By the argument in Lemma 6.14, since u is only supported on the first $\sqrt{N}$ elements, note that:

$$\|B^\dagger u\| = \|X^\dagger D^\dagger u\| \tag{6.150}$$
$$\geq \sigma_N(X)\|D^\dagger u\| \tag{6.151}$$
$$\geq \sigma_N(X)\sigma_- \tag{6.152}$$
$$\geq \sigma_- O(\sqrt{M}) \tag{6.153}$$

with probability $1 - 2\exp(-O(N))$ by Lemma 6.12

Lastly, we need to control

$$\|Aw\| \leq |Bw\| + \|Cw\| \leq (\|B\| + \|C\|)\|w\| \tag{6.154}$$

And we can write again by Lemma 6.12, with similarly high probability:

$$\|B\| = \|DX\| \tag{6.155}$$
$$\leq \|D\|\|X\| \tag{6.156}$$
$$\leq \sigma_+ \sigma_1(X) \tag{6.157}$$
$$\leq \sigma_+ O(\sqrt{M}) \tag{6.158}$$

Combining this with the bound on $\|C\|$ we derived in Lemma 6.14, and the concentration on $\|w\|$ from Lemma 6.11 we have with probability $1 - 2\exp(-O(N))$:

$$\|Aw\| \leq \left(\sigma_+ O(\sqrt{M}) + e^{-O(\sqrt{N})}\right) O(\sqrt{M}) \tag{6.159}$$

Finally we can say that with probability $1 - 2\exp(-O(N))$

$$r_0 \geq c \frac{\sigma_-}{\sigma_+ \sqrt{M}} \tag{6.160}$$

for some universal constant c.

□

6.5 Experiments

To study an experimental setup for our setting, we consider the student-teacher setup outlined above with gradient descent. We consider $N = 25$, $M = 100$, and approximate the matrix A by capping the infinite number of rows at 150, which was sufficient for $1 - \|P_A h^*\|^2 \leq 0.001$ in numerical experiments. For the link function f, we choose its only non-zero monomial coefficients to be $\alpha_3 = \alpha_4 = \alpha_5 = \frac{1}{\sqrt{3}}$. And correspondingly, g simply has $\alpha_3 = 1$ and all other coefficients at zero.

We choose for convenience an activation function such that $A_{km} = \left(\frac{N-1}{N}\right)^k a_m^k$. We make this choice because, while obeying all the assumptions required in Assumption 6.6, this choice implies that the action of A on the elementary basis vectors e_j for $1 \leq j \leq \sqrt{N}$ is approximately distributed the same. This choice means that $\|P_A h^*\|$ is less dependent on the choice of h^*, and therefore reduces the variance in our experiments when we choose h^* uniformly among unit norm vectors with support on the first $\sqrt{N}$ elements, i.e. uniformly from the complex sphere in degree $\sqrt{N}$.

Under this setup, we train full gradient descent on 50000 samples from the Vandermonde V distribution under 20000 iterations. The only parameter to be tuned is the learning rate, and we observe over the small grid of $[0.001, 0.0025, 0.005]$ that a learning rate of 0.0025 performs best for the both models in terms of probability of r reaching approximately 1, i.e. strong recovery.

As described in Theorem 6.5, we use preconditioned gradient descent using $(A^\dagger A)^{-1}$ as the preconditioner, which can be calculated once at the beginning of the algorithm and is an easy alteration to vanilla gradient descent to implement. We use the pseudoinverse for improved stability in calculating this matrix, although we note that this preconditioner doesn't introduce stability issues into the updates of our summary statistics, even in the case of gradient descent. Indeed, even if one considers the loss $L(w)$ under an empirical expectation rather than full expectation, the gradient $\nabla L(w)$ can still be seen to be written in the form $A^\dagger v$ for some vector v.

If one preconditions this gradient by $(A^\dagger A)^{-1}$, and observes that the summary statistics m and v both depend on Aw rather than w directly, it follows that the gradient update on these statistics is always of the form $A(A^\dagger A)^{-1}A^\dagger = P_A$, so even in the empirical case this preconditioner doesn't introduce exploding gradients.

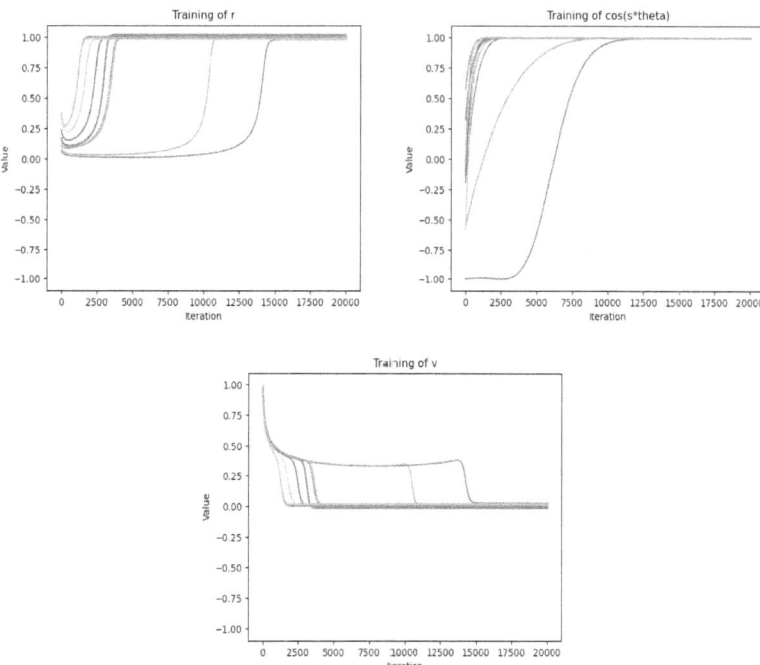

Figure 6.1: The learning trajectory, over ten independent runs, of the three summary statistics in the case of our chosen loss function L

We note that our analysis is somewhat pessimistic, as the experimental gradient descent on $L(w)$ will often achieve near perfect accuracy even if $\cos s\theta_0 < 0$. This is mainly an issue of proof technique: although $\cos s\theta$ is always increasing under the dynamics, r is necessarily decreasing for as long as $\cos s\theta$ is negative. It is quite subtle to control whether $\cos s\theta$ will become positive before r becomes extremely small, and the initialization of r is the main feature that controls the runtime of the model. However the empirical results suggest that a chance of success $> 1/2$ is possible under a more delicate analysis.

However, the analysis given in the proof of Theorem 6.8 does accurately capture the brief dip in the value of r in the initial part of training, when the regularization contributes more to the gradient than the correlation until $\cos s\theta$ becomes positive.

Because we can only run experiments on gradient descent rather than gradient flow, we observe the phenomenon of search vs descent studied in Arous et al. [2021], where the increase in the correlation term r is very slow and then abruptly increases.

www.ingramcontent.com/pod-product-compliance
Lightning Source LLC
LaVergne TN
LVHW020438070526
838199LV00063B/4778